The Believer's Armor

The Believer's Armor

by
John MacArthur, Jr.

MOODY PRESS
CHICAGO

© 1981 by
JOHN F. MACARTHUR, JR.

Moody Press Edition, 1986

All Scripture quotations, unless noted otherwise, are from the *New Scofield Reference Bible*, King James Version, copyright © 1967 by Oxford University Press, Inc. Reprinted by permission.

Library of Congress Cataloging in Publication Data

MacArthur, John F.
  The believer's armor.

  (John MacArthur's Bible studies)
    1. Christian life—Biblical teaching.   2. Bible. N.T.
Ephesians VI, 10-24—Criticism, interpretation, etc.
I. Title.   II. Series: MacArthur, John F. Bible
studies
BS2655.C4M33   1986   227'.506   85-29867
ISBN: 0-8024-5092-X

5 6 7 8 9 Printing/EP/Year 91 90 89 88

Printed in the United States of America

Contents

These Bible studies are taken from messages delivered by Pastor-Teacher John MacArthur, Jr., at Grace Community Church in Panorama City, California. The recorded messages themselves may be purchased as a series or individually. Please request the current price list by writing to:

WORD OF GRACE COMMUNICATIONS
P.O. Box 4000
Panorama City, CA 91412

Or call the following toll-free number:
1-800-55-GRACE

1
Satan's Attack on the Spirit-Filled Church

Outline

Introduction
A. Spiritual Warfare
B. Satan's Attack
  1. An awareness of the attack
    a) James 4:7
    b) 1 Peter 5:8-9
    c) 2 Corinthians 2:11
    d) Acts 20:29-31
  2. An insight into the attack
    a) The purpose of the vision
    b) The particulars of the vision
      (1) The seven lampstands
      (2) The Son of Man
      (3) The seven stars
    c) The perspective of the vision
      (1) The two commendations
      (2) The five warnings

Lesson
I. The Church at Ephesus (Rev. 2:1-6)
A. The Commendation
  1. It worked hard
  2. It hated sin
  3. It dealt with false teachers
  4. It glorified God
B. The Condemnation
C. The Command
  1. Remember
  2. Repent
  3. Repeat
II. The Church at Pergamum (Rev. 2:12-17)

1

Introduction

A. Spiritual Warfare

Ephesians 6:10-12 says, "Finally, my brethren, be strong in the Lord, and in the power of his might. Put on the whole armor of God, that ye may be able to stand against the wiles of the devil. For we wrestle not against flesh and blood, but against principalities, against powers, against the rulers of the darkness of this world, against spiritual wickedness in high places." That is the appropriate way to end the book of Ephesians. Paul is saying that if you are a true Christian, as defined in chapters 1-3, and if you are living as a true Christian should live, as defined in chapter 4-6, you can be sure you will face the enemy. It is impossible to live in the manner that the book of Ephesians outlines without having conflict with Satan. That is why the final thing you need to know is to be strong and put on the armor of God. You are in a spiritual war.

2

When I first came to Grace Community Church, my experience was like a honeymoon—a real adventure. But a few years later it was more like work. I continually had to prepare a new sermon week after week, preach it on Sunday, and start all over on Monday. Since I didn't have a backlog of sermons, I was teaching everything I knew. I had to work hard just to keep up. A few years ago I realized the honeymoon was over and that I was in a war. We all are in a battle.

That is what Paul is saying in Ephesians 6:10-12. We are to walk worthy of the vocation to which we have been called with humility and unity, not in the vanity of our mind (Eph. 4:1-3, 17). We are to put on the new man (4:24). We are to walk in love, not lust; light, not darkness; and wisdom, not foolishness (5:2-3, 8, 17). We are not to be drunk with wine but filled with the Spirit (5:18). We are not to sing worldly songs but spiritual songs (5:19). We are not to be proud and individualistic; we are to submit ourselves one to another (5:21). Wives should submit to their husbands as to the Lord (5:22). Husbands should love their wives as Christ loved the church (5:25). Children should obey their parents and parents are to nurture their children in the things of God (6:1-4). Employees and employers should have right biblical relationships (6:5-9). When we are doing all those things, we will confront the system. However, I think Christians in America have become very smug and content rather than confrontive. We have tried to accommodate the world, believing we can win the system by becoming what it is. But the opposite should be true. We have to confront the system.

B. Satan's Attack

1. An awareness of the attack

   We need to be aware that Satan is going to attack.

   a) James 4:7—"Resist the devil, and he will flee from you."

   b) 1 Peter 5:8-9—"Be sober, be vigilant, because your adversary, the devil, like a roaring lion walketh about, seeking whom he may devour; whom resist steadfast in the faith, knowing that the same afflictions are accomplished in your brethren that are in the world." Resist Satan and be aware of what he is doing.

c) 2 Corinthians 2:11—"[Beware] lest Satan should get an advantage of us; for we are not ignorant of his devices."

d) Acts 20:29-31—Paul said the following to the leaders in the Ephesian church: "For I know this, that after my departing shall grievous wolves enter in among you, not sparing the flock. Also of your own selves shall men arise, speaking perverse things" (vv. 29-30). Paul knew that wolves would attack the church from the outside and false teachers from the inside. Verse 31 says, "For the space of three years I ceased not to warn everyone night and day with tears."

Part of the church's ministry is to warn the flock. When God blesses us, multiplies our congregation, and uses us to cut a path through this evil world, Satan is going to come after us. We have to be ready; we need to have our armor on.

2. An insight into the attack

First we need to understand how Satan attacks. We do not want to be ignorant of his devices.

An Unusual Girl

One day I was called into a room where some men were being confronted by a demon-possessed girl. The demons used her mouth to speak, but the voices coming out of her were not hers. Amazing things were going on in that room. She had flipped over a desk, and she was smashing other things in the room. When I walked in the door she suddenly sat in a chair, gave me a frenzied look, and in a voice not her own, said, "Get him out! Not him! Get him out!" Those demons knew whose side I was on. They know me, and they know what God is doing in our church. They will try to stop what He's doing and will try to do so through you. The church is like a series of links in a chain—it's only as strong as its weakest link.

I believe the Lord shows how Satan attacks the church in the letters written to seven churches in Asia Minor in Revelation 2 and 3. The first church was located in Ephesus, and the others were born out of that church.

a) The purpose of the vision

4

Revelation 1:9 states that the apostle John had been exiled to the Isle of Patmos for his faith. It was there that God gave him the marvelous visions of Revelation. God wanted to reveal certain things about the church through those visions. John said, "I was in the Spirit on the Lord's Day, and heard behind me a great voice, as of a trumpet, saying, I am Alpha and Omega, the first and the last; and, What thou seest, write in a book, and send it unto the seven churches which are in Asia: unto Ephesus, and unto Smyrna, and unto Pergamum, and unto Thyatira, and unto Sardis, and unto Philadelphia, and unto Laodicea" (vv. 10-11). Those seven churches were actual historical churches. But they are also prototypes of churches that exist in all periods of church history. Each of them has unique characteristics that the Lord speaks to. There are churches in every age, including today, that could be classified as Ephesian, Smyrnaean, Pergamene, Thyatiran, Sardian, Philadelphian, or Laodicean churches.

b) The particulars of the vision

(1) The seven lampstands

In verse 12 John says, "I turned to see the voice that spoke with me. And being turned, I saw seven golden lampstands." Verse 20 indicates that the lampstands are symbolic of the seven churches. The lamps are lit—the church is to be a light to the world. It should be a light in the darkness.

(2) The Son of Man

Verse 13 says, "And in the midst of the seven lampstands [stood] one like the Son of man." He is Jesus Christ who is moving through His church. Verse 13 adds that He is clothed with a garment down to the foot. Garments like that were worn by priests, prophets, and kings. The consummation of all those roles was found in Christ. He was girded about His middle with a golden girdle; His head and His hair were white like wool and as white as snow (signifying His holiness and purity); His eyes were like a flame of fire, searching and penetrating (vv. 13-14). We see the Lord in His kingly, priestly, and prophetic garb. We see He is pure. His eyes are searching and penetrating as He evaluates the church. Verse 15 says, "His feet [are] like fine bronze, as if they burned in a furnace." Why? Because He has to judge His church. Peter said, "Judgment must begin at the house of God" (1 Pet. 4:17). Revelation 1:15 says, "His voice [is] like the sound of many waters." He has a commanding, authoritative voice.

(3) The seven stars

Verse 16 says, "He had in his right hand seven stars." What are they? Verse 20 says, "The seven stars are the angels [the ministers] of the seven churches." Christ holds the ministers in His hand as He moves among the churches to examine them. His evaluation is in Revelation 1, and the result of that evaluation is in chapters 2 and 3.

c) The perspective of the vision

What does the Lord say to the seven churches in Revelation 2-3? Five of the letters contain warnings while the other two do not.

(1) The two commendations

The churches at Smyrna and Philadelphia apparently needed no warning. The church at Smyrna was the persecuted church; the church at Philadelphia was the evangelizing, aggressive, soul-winning church. Those characteristics are wonderful preservatives for any church. When a church is persecuted, it tends to maintain its purity because its impurities drop out. You won't identify with a church that is persecuted unless you are serious about your commitment to Christ. Evangelism also has a way of purifying believers. As long as your heart is committed to aggressively reaching the lost in the world, you will tend to be outgoing rather than indifferent. The church at Philadelphia had an open door and the church at Smyrna was being tested by fires of opposition. God blessed them both.

(2) The five warnings

The other five churches were in need of serious warnings. There is a progression in the warnings.

6

The first warning is given to a church that seems to have a small problem. But that problem later develops in other churches to the point that they become apostates. A spiritual descent has occurred throughout history in many churches.

As I studied these five warnings, I became aware that the same thing can happen to our church as it has happened to thousands of churches around the world. They all began with good intentions— just like the Ephesian church. But soon the spiritual descent came and nothing spiritual remains. I've been in auditoriums in this country that could seat 4,000 people, yet there are only 150 theological liberals huddled in the front rows on a Sunday morning. In a sense God has written "Ichabod" on many churches (1 Sam. 4:21). I don't want that to happen to Grace Community Church. I'm excited over the prospect of putting a balcony in our church someday but only if I know it will be occupied by people who will hear the Word of God. I'm also excited about the prospect of building an educational center but only if it's occupied by children, young people, and adults who love the Lord Jesus Christ with all their heart, soul, mind, and strength. Otherwise, I'm not interested in a balcony or a new building.

Let's see what we need to be warned about:

Lesson

I. THE CHURCH AT EPHESUS (Rev. 2:1-6)

A. The Commendation (vv. 1-3, 6)

Verse 1 says, "Unto the angel of the church of Ephesus write: These things saith he that holdeth the seven stars in his right hand, who walketh in the midst of the seven golden lampstands." That isn't someone's opinion; that is the Son of Man, Jesus Christ, writing to His own church. In verse 2 He says, "I know thy works." A remarkable thing happened in Ephesus: The believers threw the city into confusion and chaos and overturned its system of religion (Acts 19). That little group of believers had started out as an island of purity in a sea of wretchedness. They had been so successful in

7

infiltrating and purifying parts of the city that they brought to a halt some of the most complex systems of religion in existence at that time. The Ephesian church had an incredible beginning. Who could think of a better one to begin it all than the apostle Paul? Who could think of more wonderful pastors than Apollos (with his great ability to proclaim the Word of God) and Timothy (who taught them the same things that Paul did)?

1. It worked hard

   The church at Ephesus was a hardworking church. In verse 2 Christ says, "I know thy works, and thy labor [Gk., *kopos*]." Their work was the kind that would make one sweat.

   They also were patient (Gk., *hupomonē*). They were able to endure the tough time. Ephesus wasn't an easy place to live. It was the center of the worship of Diana. The temple of Diana in Ephesus was one of the seven wonders of the world. Scores of eunuchs, thousands of priestesses and prostitutes, and many heralds and flute players created an hysterical arena of music, orgies, and drunkenness. There was so much frenzy and sexual mutilation that Heraclitus, a Greek philosopher of Ephesus during the fifth century B.C., said that the morals of the Ephesians were worse than questionable (Diogenes Laertius, *Lives of Eminent Philosophers* IX. 1). But Paul's preaching resulted in a drop in the sales of idols and brought about a riot. The people in the church at Ephesus endured in the midst of a tough city.

2. It hated sin

   In verse 2 Christ also says, "Thou canst not bear them who are evil." They were dealing with sin in the church. They wouldn't tolerate sin. When someone was doing something evil, they dealt with him. Verse 6 says, "Thou hatest the deeds of the Nicolaitans, which I also hate." Apparently the Nicolaitans following the teaching of an individual named Nicolas—a man who espoused sexual immorality. Clement of Alexandria said that the Nicolaitans "abandon themselves to pleasure like goats" (*The Miscellanies* 2:20). We can't be sure what they believed, but we do know that they practiced a licentious kind of behavior.

3. It dealt with false teachers

Verse 2 says, "Thou hast tried them who say they are apostles, and they are not." They dealt with false teachers. They had a biblical standard—a statement of faith—that they measured men by. They were doctrinally solid.

4. It glorified God

Verse 3 says, "[Thou] hast borne, and hast patience, and for my name's sake hast labored." That is the greatest motive for anything a Christian does. Glorifying God was their motive. That is the highest motive in the universe. The people in the church at Ephesus were serving in Christ's name. They labored and didn't faint.

The Ephesian church was a great church. It was doctrinally solid. The people were busy unmasking false teachers and disciplining those who were sinning. But they had one fatal flaw.

B. The Condemnation (v. 4)

In Revelation 1:14 Christ's eyes are described as "a flame of fire." The searching, penetrating eyes of Jesus Christ found a fatal flaw: "Nevertheless, I have somewhat against thee, because thou hast left thy first love" (Rev. 2:4). Love died in the church at Ephesus. It had orthodoxy and activity without love. Christ's message to that church must have hit like a thunderbolt. The church's definition of love didn't match God's. It missed the one basic thing that Jesus repeated three times to Peter. Jesus essentially said to Peter, "Before I ask you to feed My sheep, I have to ask you one thing: Do you love Me? If you say yes, then feed My sheep" (John 21:15-17). Why did Jesus need to know that? Because no one can be effective for God apart from loving the Lord with all his heart, soul, mind, and strength.

The church at Ephesus was one of the greatest churches in history. Yet the Lord's penetrating eyes found one fatal flaw. The people exchanged their hot hearts for cold orthodoxy. They carried out a biblical ministry without passion. If we ever have orthodox performance without love, we have allowed Satan to accomplish the first step in his plan to get a foothold in the church. When the honeymoon with Christ is over and you don't live your life out of overwhelming love for Him, you are in trouble. Look at your life. Is your enthusiasm for Christ still there, or is the thrill gone? Is it fair to say you don't have the same love for Christ that you used to have? If you love anything in this world (e.g., yourself, your family, leisure, money, or success) more than you love Christ, then you have lost your first love. If you're serving the Lord Jesus Christ in an orthodox way without loving Him, then you've missed the purpose of the Christian life.

C. The Command (v. 5)

If you feel you've lost your passion and love for Christ, you must do three things:

1. Remember

   Spiritual defection is usually a result of forgetfulness. Have you forgotten what your life with Christ was like before your love grew cold? Can you remember the warmth, joy, and exhilaration that was yours with Him?

2. Repent

   Revelation 2:5 says, "Remember, therefore, from where thou art fallen, and repent." If you don't love the Lord your God with all your heart, soul, mind, and strength, and your neighbor as yourself, then you have lost your first love. That is a fall from which you must repent. If the first reaction you have to a believer is anything besides love, then you've lost your first love. If the first reaction you have to Jesus Christ is anything less than a consummate love, then you've lost your first love. You need to repent.

3. Repeat

   Do the first works once more. If your service is cold and mechanical, then go back to where you started. Get back on your knees, get back to reading the Bible, get back to witnessing, get back into the fellowship, and begin praising the Lord.

The church at Ephesus didn't remember, repent, and repeat. So what Christ says would happen in verse 5 does: "I will come unto thee quickly, and will remove thy lampstand out of its place, except thou repent." The church at Ephesus died. That great evangelical orthodox, historic church went out of existence because it lost its first love.

There is a second warning to another church. (We will skip the church at Smyrna because it was the persecuted church and didn't receive a warning.)

II. THE CHURCH AT PERGAMUM (Rev. 2:12-17)

10

A. The Commendation (vv. 12-13)

Verse 12 says, "And to the angel of the church in Pergamum write: These things saith he who hath the sharp sword with two edges." The sword that is coming out of the Lord's mouth is the sword of judgment (cf. Heb. 4:12; Rev. 19:15). Then in verse 13 God says, "I know thy works, and where thou dwellest, even where Satan's throne is; and thou holdest fast my name, and hast not denied my faith, even in those days in which Antipas was my faithful martyr, who was slain among you, where Satan dwelleth." The Lord is saying, "I know everything about you. My searching, penetrating gaze reveals all things. I know your works. I know you're active in ministry. And I know that you are where Satan's throne is, which is a rough place to be."

A Tough City

Pergamos was a tough city. It was the center of the worship of Caesar and of Zeus, the greatest of all the Greek deities. A huge altar to Zeus had been built in Pergamos in the shape of a throne. Some commentators believe that the throne of Satan mentioned in verse 13 is a reference to the altar of Zeus, the most famous altar in the world. But Pergamos also had its own god by the name of Asclepius. He was considered the god of healing. He has always been associated with snakes. There was a medical school in the temple of Asclepius. The snake that appears as the modern symbol of the physician comes from Greek mythology and the god Asclepius. Nonpoisonous snakes crawled all over the floor in the temple. People who were ill would lie on the floor so the snakes could crawl on them. Wherever the snakes touched them, they would supposedly be healed.

It was hard being a part of a little group of Christians in the midst of such a terrible pagan society. So Christ in effect says, "I know you dwell where Satan's throne is. I know you hold fast to My name and have not denied the faith. Some of you have even died, including our dear brother Antipas." There is no reason for not naming the name of Christ, even when you are living in a tough city, environment, or time in the world. There's no reason to lower God's standards, because He doesn't change them. He knows life can be tough, but that doesn't change His standards.

B. The Condemnation (vv. 14-15)

Even though the people in the church at Pergamos had endured great difficulties, suffered martyrdom, worked for the Lord, and upheld His name, verse 14 says, "But I have a few things against thee." What were those things?

1. The teaching of Balaam (v. 14)

Verse 14 continues, "Thou hast there them that hold the doctrine of Balaam, who taught Balak to cast a stumbling block before the children of Israel, to eat things sacrificed unto idols, and to commit fornication." Balaam led the children of Israel to intermarry with pagans and to follow their idolatrous practices. They compromised with the pagan systems. The same kind of problem had occurred in the church at Pergamos—the people were compromising with the world. I don't know if Christians were actually intermarrying with non-Christians, but the church at Pergamos had begun to court the world and to indulge in worldly things. The people were violating 2 Corinthians 6:14-15, 17: "What communion hath light with darkness? And what concord hath Christ with Belial? . . . Come out from among them, and be ye separate, saith the Lord, and touch not the unclean thing." But it was too late; they had let the world come in. Now they were doing what the world wanted them to do.

Accommodating the World's Opinions

It amazes me how the church in America today tries to copy the world in so many ways. If the world's view of the family, the woman, or the homosexual changes, the church accommodates that. We have a tendency to jump on the bandwagon of everything that the world does. We want to identify with it. That is shocking! The church becomes materialistic because the world is materialistic. The church becomes preoccupied with entertainment because the world is preoccupied with entertainment. Let me give you an illustration:

Although there has been a steady rise in the number of people who call themselves born-again in the last ten years, there has been a corresponding steady decline in the number of church members, because many of them aren't attending churches. An article I read said that the rise of what has become known as the "electronic church" is the primary reason many people don't identify with the local church (William F. Fore, "The Electronic Church," *Ministry* [January

1979]). They sit at home in front of their televisions, and the church comes to them. They don't have to get dressed and leave the house—it's a perfect environment. But it's only another part of the fantasy. Television is fantasy, and our world wants to live in that fantasy. The church that comes into our homes is a perfect church. The music is unbelievable. It has a grand orchestra and great singers. The preacher gives a perfect message. In the fantasy church you never have to sit next to anyone you don't like, no one ever disturbs you, and you don't have to find a place to park. All you have to do is send them a little money now and then to ease your conscience, and they will tell you that you're winning the world. They may send you something you can plaster on your wall to prove how sacrificial you are. What a sad commentary on the church.

The electronic church is built on entertainment. It duplicates the very things in the world that the church has always condemned. The electronic church is a mere expression of cultural religion, copying the value, glitter, and trappings of the very values and kinds of success that we as Christians profess to reject. Let's live in the real world. When the church is so smug and comfortable in its compromising position, it falls into the world's fantasy.

2. The doctrine of the Nicolaitans (v. 15)

    Revelation 2:15 says, "So hast thou also them that hold the doctrine of the Nicolaitans, which thing I hate." The church in Pergamos decided it could court the world by drawing a little of it into the church. The people thought it would be acceptable to allow for some immorality. In one case I know of, an elder of a church told me that two fellow elders exchanged wives. The pastor thought the church shouldn't do anything about it because it might upset the congregation. When a church begins to compromise by tolerating sin, its message might still be the same, but their compromise eats away at its foundation like termites.

C. The Command (vv. 16-17)

    In verse 16 Christ says, "Repent, or else I will come unto thee quickly, and will fight against them with the sword of my mouth." Do you know how Satan attacks the church? He starts very subtly by causing us to lose our first love. Then suddenly, we begin to compromise with the world. Our lack of love for God is the easiest way to be led into compromise.

13

If you really love God and the Lord Jesus Christ with all your heart, soul, mind, and strength, your desire—above all things—will be to maintain His absolute honor. To do that, you can't compromise with the world's system. But as soon as your love cools, it becomes easier to fall into the trap of the system. If you don't love God, you will tend to love what's around you.

III. THE CHURCH AT THYATIRA (Rev. 2:18-29)

A. The Commendation (vv. 18-19)

Revelation 2:18-19 says, "And unto the angel of the church in Thyatira write: These things saith the Son of God, who hath his eyes like a flame of fire, and his feet are like fine bronze. I know thy works, and love, and service, and faith, and thy patience, and thy works; and the last to be more than the first." The people were getting better in those characteristics. It was an active church.

B. The Condemnation (vv. 20-23)

The church in Pergamos may have married the world, but the church at Thyatira was celebrating its anniversary. Ephesus lost its first love, Pergamos compromised with the world, and Thyatira tolerated sin. The floodgate to sin was open.

1. Thyatira's tolerance of Jezebel

In spite of all their works, love, service, faith, and patience, verse 20 says, "I have a few things against thee, because thou allowest that woman, Jezebel, who calleth herself a prophetess, to teach and to seduce my servants to commit fornication, and to eat things sacrificed unto idols." The people in that church had love, service, and faith, but they let the church become victimized by a false teacher. They allowed sin to come in. People were actually committing fornication. A woman called Jezebel was seducing the people of the church into the idol worship of the day. Idolatry during those eras of history involved sexual activity. So the people in the church at Thyatira were having a great time getting involved in the filth of the world.

When couples come in for premarital counseling and are asked if they have gone to bed together, it's a rare day when a couple says no. Is that shocking to you? We live in a vile and evil world. People are drawn into sin when they're not aware of what's going on and when they don't build up their defenses by walking in the Spirit.

2. Christ's intolerance of Jezebel

God was patient with Jezebel. Christ said, "I gave her space to repent of her fornication, and she repented not. Behold, I will cast her into a bed" (vv. 21-22). Christ was saying, "Since she likes beds so much, I'll put her in one. If she wants to commit fornication, I'll put her into a fornicating situation." Verse 23 indicates that the bed would be a bed of death because He would kill her children. The people who listened to Jezebel were designated as her children, and Christ planned to kill them. Verse 23 also says, "And all the churches shall know that I am he who searcheth the minds and hearts; and I will give unto every one of you according to your works." The Lord will judge His church. Don't think you can be a believer and avoid God's chastening for sin. Verse 22 indicates that those who followed Jezebel's teaching committed adultery with her. Why was that considered adultery? Because the believer is married to Christ, and fooling around with idols and sexual activity is a form of adultery. So Christ tells churches that tolerate sin to repent. If they don't, He will kill them.

C. The Command (vv. 24-29)

To those who weren't involved in Jezebel's sin, the Lord said, "I will put upon you no other burden. But that which ye have already, hold fast till I come" (vv. 24-25). But those who are evil will receive judgment.

The church at Thyatira tolerated sin. Many churches today do that very thing. They don't want to deal with sin, and they don't want to confront anyone. I am often asked, "Do you actually discipline people in your church?" We do because the Bible says to. People who ask me that often respond, "We don't want to do that because we might offend someone." So they compromise with the world instead. The destruction of the church is a spiral descent. It starts with a loss of love. Then when you don't love the Lord anymore, you're soon willing to compromise. After you compromise for a while, you become tolerant, and sin floods the church.

IV. THE CHURCH AT SARDIS (Rev. 3:1-6)

A. The Condemnation (v. 1)

The church at Sardis was content with its programs. The light was gone. A church that tolerates sin becomes a degenerate church. Christ said, "I know thy works, that thou hast a name that thou livest, and art dead" (v. 1). Do you know that Sardis was one of the greatest cities in the ancient world? Its greatest king was named Croesus. When we want to indicate how rich someone is, we sometimes say he is as rich as Croesus. The city of Sardis was synonymous with wealth, but that city and its church went out of existence because it was characterized by a degenerate, dead church.

B. The Command (vv. 2-3, 5-6)

In verse 2 Christ says, "Be watchful, and strengthen the things which remain, that are ready to die." They were either dead or ready to die. All they had left was form. In *The Rime of the Ancient Mariner* Samuel Coleridge said, "Corpses man the ship; dead men pull the oars; dead men hoist the sails; dead men steer the vessel" (Santa Fe, N. Mex.: Gannon, William, 1970). Things were functioning in the church, but everyone was dead. That's what happens when a church becomes a group of activities and a series of programs. There are classes and activities for the kids, young people, and adults. Everyone is busy, but there's no life. God's not there. In a sense God has written "Ichabod" on that church (1 Sam. 4:21).

The sequence of the destruction of the church is easy to see: You lose your first love. That leads to compromise with the world. Then sin floods in; you begin to give in to it and tolerate it. When sin completely takes over the church, spiritual life is choked out, leaving a dead church. Like Samson, it is busy moving around—it just doesn't have any strength. It is a victim. That is why Christ said, "Remember, therefore, how thou hast received and heard, and hold fast, and repent. If, therefore, thou shalt not watch, I will come on thee as a thief, and thou shalt not know what hour I will come upon thee" (Rev. 3:3).

C. The Commendation (v. 4)

In verse 4 the Lord says, "Thou hast a few names even in Sardis that have not defiled their garments, and they shall walk with me in white; for they are worthy." There were still a few true believers left in the church. Ephesus was a tremendous church, but the people began to lose their first

16

love. In Sardis only a few remained.

The next step in the descent of the church comes as Satan attacks with his final blow.

V. THE CHURCH AT LAODICEA (Rev. 3:14-21)

Our Lord warned the church that left its first love, compromised with the world, tolerated sin, and was content with its programs. Now he warns the church that is apostate—the church that is not a church.

A. The Condemnation (vv. 14-17)

1. Lukewarmness

   Christ said, "And unto the angel of the church of the Laodiceans write: These things saith the Amen, the faithful and true witness, the beginning of the creation of God. I know thy works, that thou art neither cold nor hot; I would thou wert cold or hot" (Rev. 3:14-15). The word *cold* is used here to mean indifferent to the gospel, unsaved. The one who is cold is not hypocritical; he is just uninterested and unconcerned. The Lord preferred that the people in the church at Laodicea be at least like that, or even better that they be hot—believing, saved, redeemed. But they were playing at Christianity. Hypocrisy nauseates Christ. He said, "Because thou art lukewarm, and neither cold nor hot, I will spew thee out of my mouth" (v. 16). He tries to draw people who are cold to Himself by preaching to them through His messengers. He embraces those who are hot. But He spits people who are lukewarm out of His mouth. They are the hypocrites. And the church at Laodicea is the hypocritical, phony church—the church that is no church.

2. Self-deception

   You will find theological liberalism in the Laodicean church today. It exists under the guise of Christianity, but its followers deny the Bible, the deity of Jesus Christ, and other great tenants of the Christian faith. This is the church of the humanists. When you ask them about their church they don't say, "We are seeing God's Word prevail. We are seeing people redeemed." Instead they say, "I am rich, and increased with goods, and have need of nothing" (v. 17). In other words, "Look at us. We're successful! We've got a big organization and a lot of

17

money!" There are huge churches around the world— great denominations and massive religious systems that fall into this category. They've got all the money and all the trappings, but they are apostate. One day the Lord will spew them out of His mouth. In verse 17 He adds, "Thou art wretched, and miserable, and poor, and blind, and naked."

B. The Command (vv. 18-21)

In verse 18, Christ says, "I counsel thee to buy of me gold tried in the fire, that thou mayest be rich; and white raiment, that thou mayest be clothed, and that the shame of thy nakedness do not appear; and anoint thine eyes with salve, that thou mayest see." He is saying to them, "You don't have a right evaluation of yourselves." Then in verse 19 He says, "As many as I love [Gk., *phileō*], I rebuke and chasten; be zealous, therefore, and repent."

Conclusion

Do you see what our Lord Jesus Christ warns us about? The church can eventually descend into the pit of apostasy. The church at Ephesus went out of existence because it lost its first love. When that happens, a church can easily compromise with the world. Many people won't come to church just to study the Word of God or to pray. Many people want to be entertained. Sometimes we tend to think, "If we just had a big production, everyone would come to church." But if we say that we're going to study the Word of God, only the faithful few come. Often churches have exercised wrong thinking by entertaining the saints and copying the world. That's a compromise. The church then begins to tolerate sin and marries the world. Finally, it becomes satisfied with material riches but really has nothing—it's dead. That's how Satan attacks the church. But there are preservatives.

A. Evangelism Preserves the Church

This is a description of the Philadelphia church: "These things saith he that is holy, he that is true, he that hath the key of David, he that openeth, and no man shutteth; and shutteth, and no man openeth. I know thy works; behold, I have set before thee an open door, and no man can shut it" (Rev. 3:7-8). Christ is saying, "I opened the door for you to reach the world, and it's wide open." As long as the church is committed to go through that door and take Christ to the world no matter what happens—including the presence of the synagogue of Satan or the time of trouble—Satan can't touch the church. Evangelism is a preservative. It throws us out of our shells; it helps us step beyond our inhibitions and crucify pride.

B. Persecution Preserves the Church

The Lord says this about the Smyrnaean church: "I know thy works, and tribulation, and poverty" (Rev. 2:9). They were being blasphemed. But He says, "Fear none of those things which thou shalt suffer. Behold, the devil shall cast some of you into prison, that ye may be tried, and ye shall have tribulation ten days; be thou faithful unto death, and I will give thee a crown of life" (v. 10).

Beloved, if we confront the world and take what comes, and if we are aggressive to win people to Christ, we can stand with the churches at Smyrna and Philadelphia and not fall into the trap of the other five churches. May God help us to be warned about Satan's attacks.

Focusing on the Facts

1. What can you be sure will happen when you live as a true Christian should live (see p. 2)?
2. What should Christians do instead of accommodating the world's system (see p. 3)?
3. What is one important aspect of the church's ministry regarding Satan (see p. 4)?
4. Name the seven churches the apostle John wrote to in Revelation 2-3. What is significant about those churches (Rev. 1:10-11; see p. 5)?
5. What do the seven golden lampstands symbolize in John's vision (Rev. 1:12, 20; see p. 5)?
6. Whom did John see in his vision? Describe Him. What do the descriptions John gave of Him symbolize (Rev. 1:13-15; see p. 5)?
7. What do the seven stars symbolize in John's vision (Rev. 1:16; see p. 6)?
8. Explain why the churches at Smyrna and Philadelphia needed no warning from the Lord (see p. 6).
9. Describe the initial effect that the believers in Ephesus had on the city (Acts 19; see pp. 7-8).

10. Why was Ephesus a difficult city for a Christian to live in (see p. 8)?
11. Who were the Nicolaitans? What did the Ephesian church think of them (Rev. 2:6; see p. 8)?
12. What is the greatest motive for anything that a Christian does (Rev. 2:3; see p. 9)?
13. What fatal flaw in the church of Ephesus had Christ discovered? Explain (Rev. 2:4; see p. 9).
14. What does every Christian need to have to be effective in serving God (see p. 9)?
15. What are the three things a Christian should do if he thinks he has lost his love for Christ? Explain (Rev. 2:5; see p. 10).
16. What finally happened to the church at Ephesus (Rev. 2:5; see p. 10)?
17. What does the sword that comes out of the Lord's mouth in Rev. 2:12 symbolize (see p. 11)?
18. Describe the city of Pergamos (see p. 11).
19. Why is there no reason for Christians to lower biblical standards, even when they are involved in a difficult situation or environment (see p. 11)?
20. What was the main problem that existed in the church at Pergamos (Rev. 2:14; see p. 12)?
21. What are some ways that many churches today accommodate the world's views (see pp. 12-13)?
22. What is the easiest way for Christians to allow themselves to be led into compromise (see p. 13)?
23. Even though the church at Thyatira was commended for their love, service, faith, and patience, what did they allow to happen (Rev. 2:20; see p. 15)?
24. What did the Lord plan to do if those who had followed the teaching of Jezebel didn't repent (Rev. 2:21-23; see p. 15)?
25. What eventually happens to a church that continually tolerates sin (Rev. 3:1; see p. 15)?
26. Define the terms *cold, hot,* and *lukewarm* as Christ uses them in Revelation 3:14-15. Why did He wish that those in the Laodicean church were either cold or hot (see p. 17)?
27. Describe how theological liberalism might manifest itself in the church today (Rev. 3:17; see pp. 17-18).
28. How does evangelism function as a preservative (see pp. 18-19)?

Pondering the Principles

1. Examine your life. Is your enthusiasm for Christ still present, or is the thrill of knowing Him gone? Do you love any of the

following more than you love Christ: yourself, your family, leisure, money, or success? If you do, then you have left your first love for Christ. Based on Revelation 2:5, what do you need to remember? What do you need to repent of? And what do you need to repeat? Start improving your relationship to Christ today.

2. Have you ever compromised your Christian testimony in the world? Have you ever watered down a biblical truth to allow yourself some worldly indulgence? Give some examples. Read James 4:4 and 1 John 2:15. What does God say about those who ally themselves with the world? Read Romans 5:1-11. What are some of the characteristics of the relationship God began with you as a result of your salvation? As a result, do you desire to be a friend or an enemy of God? What worldly ties do you have to give up to be what God wants you to be?

3. Jesus opened a door for the church at Philadelphia to reach the world. What are some practical ways you can be more active in sharing your faith? Are you looking for doors that Christ has opened? How many doors have you missed—or were simply unwilling to go through? Make the commitment to reflect the attributes of Jesus Christ. Follow the practical suggestions you have made, and be consistent to apply them daily.

2
The Believer's Warfare—Part 1

Outline

Introduction
A. Our Position
B. Our Practice
C. Our Warfare
   1. Identified
   2. Intensified
      a) An unending conflict
      b) An unbending confidence
D. Our Enemy
   1. The physical enemy
   2. The supernatural enemy

Lesson
I. The Preparation
A. Our Strength in Christ
B. Our Victory in Christ
C. Our Power in Christ
   1. Its availability
      a) Resurrection power
      b) Glorious power
      c) Dependable power
         (1) Man's vulnerability
         (2) Man's invulnerability
   2. Its appropriation
   3. Its assurance
II. The Armor
III. The Enemy
A. Satan Himself
   1. His background
   2. His works
   3. His titles
   4. His character

Introduction

Ephesians 6:10-13 says, "Finally, my brethren, be strong in the Lord, and in the power of his might. Put on the whole armor of God, that ye may be able to stand against the wiles of the devil. For we wrestle not against flesh and blood, but against principalities, against powers, against the rulers of the darkness of this world, against spiritual wickedness in high places. Wherefore, take unto you the whole armor of God, that ye may be able to withstand in the evil day, and having done all, to stand." Let me briefly set the context of this passage.

A. Our Position

In the book of Ephesians, Paul presents the great realities of being in Christ—what it means to be a believer, to belong to God, to have the indwelling Spirit of God, to become adopted into God's family, and to stand in Him. Those things describe the position of the believer before God. His identity and character are defined by his relationship to Jesus Christ. The first three chapters of Ephesians describe the believer's position. It indicates that we have been blessed "with all spiritual blessings in heavenly places" (Eph. 1:3). We have received adoption, love, predestination, forgiveness, enlightenment, knowledge, understanding, and power. We have been removed from the dominion of Satan and placed into the kingdom of Christ (Eph. 2:5-6). We have been made to perform good works that God has previously ordained (Eph. 2:10). We have been delivered out of a worldly life-style and ushered into a new dominion: a union with God, Christ, and the Spirit, and therefore, a union with every other believer. We think, feel, talk, and act differently than we did before. That has all been accomplished according to God's purpose through the mystery of the church. He has made us one in Jesus Christ and filled us with the power that raised Christ from the dead (Eph. 1:19-20).

B. Our Practice

In Ephesians 4-6 the apostle Paul discusses our practice—how we are to live according to the standards God has set.

A Car and a Map

The idea of the Christian's practice can be illustrated by a car. The first three chapters of Ephesians describe the car: its engine and its capabilities. The second three chapters are the road map the car is to follow. The first three chapters define believers as high-powered individuals; the second three chapters show them where to go with their power. The ignition switch is represented by the strengthening of the Spirit in the inner man. As the Spirit fills and controls the believer, the power plant is turned on. He then can begin to move out in obedience to follow the road map that God has given.

Christians are to live in a way that is different from the world. We are to have a worthy walk—a walk of unity, love, light, wisdom, and Spirit-led direction. Our relationships, our songs, our marriages, our families, and our employment situations are to be different (Eph. 5:18-6:9). In all those areas God has provided unique standards by which the believer is to function in the world.

C. Our Warfare

1. Identified

You have all the resources, power, and principles to live the Christian life. But there is still one thing you need to know: It will not be easy to live this life. It is on that note that Paul chooses to end his letter. Don't take anything for granted. Just because you know how you should operate on the job doesn't guarantee that you'll pull it off. Even though you may know how you are to conduct yourself and your family doesn't mean you will do so. You may know the truths about resurrection power, but that doesn't mean you're going to apply them. You also may know what God teaches about marriage, but that doesn't guarantee you'll see the fulfillment of it. Even though power is available to follow godly principles, the enemy wants to withstand any good thing that God sets out to do. He will attempt to thwart God's divine purpose for your life.

The best word to use to define the Christian life is *warfare*. That is how Paul refers to the Christian life in Ephesians 6. In fact, at the end of his life, Paul said that he fought a good fight (2 Tim. 4:7). In speaking of his ministry he said that he fought "not as one that beateth the air" (1 Cor. 9:26). He told Timothy to be a soldier who endures hardship (2 Tim. 2:3).

2. Intensified

Scripture repeatedly pictures the Christian life as warfare.

a) An unending conflict

The initial experience of Christ's ministry was war with Satan. The conflict began after Jesus had fasted forty days. Satan subtly tempted Him three times (Matt. 4:1-11). Christ's ministry ended in a similiar way. Satan besieged Him in the Garden of Gethsemane. Jesus began to sweat, as it were, great drops of blood (Luke 22:44). Those two events indicate that you will be in the same battle, whether you are at the beginning of your Christian life or the end. If you think it will get easier, you're wrong. Jesus had conflict at the beginning of His ministry, but He didn't sweat great drops of blood until the conflict in the garden. If anything, there was an intensification of effort on the part of the enemy as Christ came closer to accomplishing His goals.

When I was young, someone told me, "You ought to begin to witness because the more you do it, the easier it gets." That statement isn't true! The more effective you become, the harder Satan works. People have said, "You've been preaching so long; it must be easy." It isn't any easier now than it was before. Sometimes it's more difficult. Satan wants to keep me from preaching. I fight to find the time to study more often than I ever did before. Sometimes I study early in the morning, late at night, or whenever I can. There are many things Satan tries to do to undermine the authority of one who teaches the Word of God. The Christian life never stops being a war.

b) An unbending confidence

A certain sense of weariness accompanies a great sense of accomplishment in the warfare. However, the longer you fight the battle, the greater the string of victories will be; the greater the string of victories, the greater your confidence in God will be. The more you know that God is going to see you through some trial, the more thrilling it is for you as you see His power at work. I can understand what the apostle John means when he says that after the saints die, they rest from all their labors (Rev. 14:13). I think about heaven in those terms sometimes. But as long as I'm still here, I want to be in the midst of the battle.

In 1 Corinthians 16:8-9 the apostle Paul says, "I will tarry at Ephesus until Pentecost. For a great door, and effectual, is opened unto me, and there are many adversaries." He wanted to stay because the war was hottest in Ephesus. Many Christians say, "I've got to get out of this ministry; it's too difficult. I've got to find an easier one." Many men are ready to leave the pastorate as soon as it gets tough. The Christian life never ceases to be warfare. Living for Christ is not like waltzing through a meadow picking daisies; it is like walking through a mine field with snipers firing at you! And you can't see the snipers because they belong to a supernatural realm.

D. Our Enemy

This life is a war, and the enemy is hell-bent on the destruction of every divine purpose. The believer has to view his life in that manner. We are sons and servants, but we are also soldiers. In 2 Corinthians 10:4-5 Paul says, "For the weapons of our warfare are not carnal, but mighty through God . . . casting down imaginations, and every high thing that exalteth itself against the knowledge of God, and bringing into captivity every thought to the obedience of Christ." We are fighting in a war that is not simply physical, but it can have that element.

1. The physical enemy

The battle can come through human beings. It came to Jesus through the persecution of men (in the form of spit, mockery, cursing, blows to the face, nails in the hands, and a spear in the side). The battle came to the apostles in the form of being killed for the sake of Christ. It may even come to us in those ways if we continue to preach Jesus Christ faithfully to an increasingly godless humanistic society.

27

2. The supernatural enemy

Beyond the hatred and persecution Christians receive from people, there is a domain of spiritual beings at war with the believer. They simply use the physical world as a means to their ends. Men don't hate Christ as much as Satan hates Christ. He uses men as his pawns. Satan is the force behind the warfare. We face an enemy who is strong, clever, deceptive, and subtle. If we are ever to know the fullness of the Christian life, we must listen to what Paul says in Ephesians 6:10-18. We can't be foolish enough to think we won't run into any opposition. As long as we endeavor to live in God's kingdom on God's terms, Satan will do his best to withstand us.

As we look at Ephesians 6:10-13, let me share with you concerning the preparation, the armor, the enemy, the battle, and the victory.

Lesson

I. THE PREPARATION (v. 10)

You don't want the battle to begin when you are unprepared. That's why preparation must occur first. In verse 10 Paul says, "Finally, my brethren, be strong in the Lord, and in the power of his might." This is a general principle of life: Depend on the strength of God.

A. Our Strength in Christ

Paul uses the word *in* twice in verse 10: "Be strong *in* the Lord, and *in* the power of his might" (emphasis added). Throughout the book of Ephesians we are told that we are "in Christ." We are one with Him—His life is our life, His power is our power, and His truth is our truth. In Christ we are strong. No matter how strong our enemy is, Christ's strength is superior.

The church at Philadelphia was one of two churches that did not receive condemnation from Christ in His message to the seven churches (Rev. 2-3). It was a righteous community of faith. Our Lord said that He had set an open door before them (Rev. 3:8). This church was reaching out and was blessed by God. Continuing in verse 8 Christ says, "Thou hast a little strength." God is so much more powerful than Satan that even a little of His strength is enough to overcome all the church's enemies. First John 4:4 says, "Greater is he that is in you, that he that is in the world." The smallest amount of divine power can overcome the greatest amount of hell's power. That strength is ours in the Lord. Philippians 4:13 says, "I can do all things through Christ, who strengtheneth me." I believe we have that resource. To deny it is to deny a fundamental reality of the Christian life.

B. Our Victory in Christ

Christ dealt a death blow to Satan at the cross. Hebrews 2:14 says, "Through death he [destroyed] him that had the power of death." All we have to do is enter into that victory. If Christ defeated Satan at the cross, and if I was in Christ when He did so, then I also defeated Satan at the cross. Therefore, as Satan is now subject to Christ, he is also subject to me. He is a vanquished foe who can lay no just claim to a believer. Romans 8:33 says, "Who shall lay any thing to the charge of God's elect? Shall God that justifieth?" If God declared me just through the victory He has won in Jesus Christ, then that victory is also mine. Satan has no power to withstand the resurrection power that dwells in the life of every believer. Yes, we are in a war, but there is no reason to lose or be afraid because divine resources belong to us.

When Timothy was a young man in the ministry, he had grown fearful and timid. He had been tempted by the lust that often tempts young men, and had been besieged by people who propagated false doctrine. As a result, he was allowing himself to be inundated by his own fearfulness and became ashamed of the testimony of Jesus Christ and his beloved companion in the gospel, the apostle Paul. It was in the midst of these terrible feelings of timidity and fear that Paul said, "Be strong in the grace that is in Christ Jesus" (2 Tim. 2:1). There was no reason for his fear because he could claim the strength that was his in Christ. In 2 Timothy 1:7 Paul says, "For God hath not given us the spirit of fear, but of power, and of love, and of a sound mind." No Christian at any time in his life should ever think that he has lost the battle to the enemy. God has given us our resource for victory in Christ: "Now unto him who is able to do exceedingly abundantly above all that we ask or think, according to the power that worketh in us" (Eph. 3:20).

C. Our Power in Christ

We know we're going to win the war because Christ has gained the victory, so there is no need to lose the battles along the way. But there are two things we need to know: First, we have to have our strength in the Lord; second, we have to put on the armor of God.

Do We Need Christian Exorcisms?

Today many Christians are concerned about how to deliver each other from demons. As a result, there is much of what is known as Christian exorcism taking place. That concept is totally foreign to Scripture. There is no incident recorded in Scripture of a demon being cast out of a believer. Only two things are important to remember when dealing with Satan: The strength of the Lord and the provision that God has made for every believer in Christ. Why are rituals and exorcisms unnecessary? Because we already have the necessary resources in Christ.

1. Its availability

    a) Resurrection power

    Ephesians 1:19-21 says, "And what is the exceeding greatness of his power toward us who believe, according to the working of his mighty power, which he wrought in Christ, when he raised him from the dead, and set him at his own right hand in the heavenly places, far above all principality, and power, and might, and dominion, and every name that is named, not only in this age, but also in that which is to come." What kind of power do we have? The power that conquered death, that exalted Christ to the right hand of God and put every angel and demon in the universe under His feet. Every believer has resources within him to deal with Satan, no matter what onslaughts the devil may bring. But there still are two conditions: (1) The believer's strength must be in the Lord and not in himself and (2) he must utilize the armor—the provision God has made for him.

    b) Glorious power

    In Colossians 1:10-11 Paul prays "that ye might walk worthy of the Lord unto all pleasing, being fruitful in every good work, and increasing in the knowledge of God; strengthened with all might, according to his glorious power." Verse 13 says that Christ, "who hath delivered us from the power of darkness, and hath translated us into the kingdom of his dear Son," has given us that power. There is not one believer who cannot deal with Satan in terms of the resurrection power that is available in Christ.

c) Dependable power

(1) Man's vulnerability

In 1 Corinthians 10:12 Paul says, "Wherefore, let him that thinketh he standeth take heed lest he fall." Do you know when you are vulnerable? When you think you're not, when you think you have all the information you need, or when you think you can handle Satan by yourself. But the point of 1 Corinthians 10:12 is this: When you think you can, you can't.

(2) Man's invulnerability

When you depend on God, there is nothing Satan can do that would cause you to lose the victory. First Corinthians 10:13 says, "There hath no temptation taken you but such as is common to man; but God is faithful." Notice that the availability of the power is dependent on the faithful character of God. Verse 13 continues, "God is faithful, who will not permit you to be tempted above that ye are able, but will, with the temptation, also make the way to escape, that ye may be able to bear it." There will never be a time when you can't overcome Satan, but you must depend on Christ. In fact, His resources are most available to you when you are weakest. In 2 Corinthians 12:9-10 Paul says, "My strength is made perfect in weakness. . . . For when I am weak, then am I strong." When you know you can't handle a situation and depend on Him, He will handle it for you.

To Fight or Not to Fight

Suppose you are a soldier in the army. You are on guard duty watching for the approach of an enemy army. Suddenly, you see the enemy approaching your fort. What should you do? Should you leave the fort and start firing on the enemy with your gun? If you're smart, you won't. Guards don't fight the war; they tell the commander that the enemy is attacking.

> When Satan attacks, don't fight; report to the Commander. David said this to Goliath: "The battle is the Lord's" (1 Sam. 17:47). Let the Lord fight the battles.

We need to know that power is available. Ephesians 6:10 tells us we can "be strong in the Lord, and in the power of his might." There is no reason to feel defeated. A believer is never so much in bondage to Satan that he can't escape if he has confidence in the power of God and wears the armor of God. The Holy Spirit said to King Jehoshaphat, "The battle is not yours, but God's" (2 Chron. 20:15). That's great to know because I wouldn't want to get into spiritual warfare without being able to see the enemy or know how he operated. When temptation comes, I'm to report to the Commander in Chief and ask Him to purge my life and make me a righteous vessel. In His righteousness I stand fearless, protected by God.

2. Its appropriation

3. Its assurance

(These points are discussed in the next lesson. See pp. 45-47).

II. THE ARMOR (v. 11a)

"Put on the whole armor of God."

A believer needs to have his armor on. It doesn't do him any good otherwise. A believer needs to depend on God's power and be obedient in putting on the available armor.

The phrase "put on" means "to put on once and for all." The armor isn't like a game uniform you put on at game time; you put the armor on once and leave it on the rest of your life. You don't lay your armor down until you meet the Lord. If you don't have it on, you are vulnerable at any time. Paul was probably chained to a Roman soldier as he wrote Ephesians, and he saw in the Roman soldier's uniform the perfect illustration of how the believer is to be prepared to fight the enemy. In Ephesians 6:14-17 Paul speaks about the armor: The loins are girded about with truthfulness, the body is covered with the breastplate of righteousness, the feet are shod with the preparation of the gospel of peace, the head is covered with the helmet of salvation, and the hands hold the shield of faith and the sword of the Spirit, which is the Word of God. The basic necessity for the believer is this: Depend on the Lord and put on the armor—and leave it on. Christians are very gullible if they think that merely knowing the

32

facts will protect them. The armor is a requirement for righteous living. If you want to be a winner in the Christian life, then put on the armor, because you will be facing battles until the day you die.

III. THE ENEMY (vv. 11b-12)

A. Satan Himself (v. 11b)

"That ye may be able to stand against the wiles of the devil."

We know we have the power of the Lord. When we are obedient to put on the armor, we're ready to depend on divine power and stand against the wiles of the devil. The believer must stand because Satan will attack him. You don't need to go find the devil; he will find you. I worry about people who seek out demons because they are delving into an area where they have no information. When you concern yourself with the power of God and the armor, God will take care of the enemy. Just stand firm. The Bible never tells us to attack the devil; it tells us to resist him and he will flee (James 4:7).

1. His background

Who is the enemy? He is the devil. Many people say, "There is no devil. He's just a Halloween costume, a figure with a pointed tail, two little horns, and a pitchfork." But that is not what the Bible says. Isaiah 14:12-17 and Ezekiel 28:11-19 tell us that the devil was originally called Lucifer and was the greatest angel and highest being God ever made. He was the anointed cherub who sparkled with all the jewels of heaven. However, Lucifer wanted to be like God. As a result of his sin of pride, he was thrown out of heaven. Revelation 12:3-4 says that he took a third of the angels with him. It is Lucifer, the fallen angel, who leads a host of one third of all created angels. They are the demonic enemy.

Jesus believed in the devil (Matt. 4:1-11; John 12:31; 14:30; 16:11). Paul talked about him (1 Cor. 7:5) and so did Peter (1 Pet. 5:8) and James (James 4:7).

2. His works

The devil tempted Eve (Gen. 3:1-6) and Christ (Matt. 4:1-11). He perverts God's Word (Matt. 4:6) and opposes God's work (Zech. 3:1-2). He hinders God's servants (1 Thess. 2:18) and the gospel (2 Cor. 4:3-4). He snares the wicked (1 Tim. 3:6-7). He desires to control the nations of the earth (Rev. 16:13-14). He is described as an angel of light in 2 Corinthians 11:14. He fought with Michael (Jude 9). He brought sin into the world (Gen. 3:13). He now has the whole world lying in his lap (1 John 5:18-19). In Genesis 2:15 God tells Adam and Eve to watch over the Garden of Eden. Why? There must have been some element of danger or there wouldn't have been such a command. Imminent danger soon revealed itself when the serpent tempted man to fall.

3. His titles

The Bible calls the devil "the anointed cherub" (Ezek. 28:14), "the prince of this world" (John 16:11), "the prince of the power of the air" (Eph. 2:2), "the god of this age" (2 Cor. 4:4), and "the prince of demons" (Luke 11:15, NIV*). Fifty-two times he is called by his most common title, "Satan," which means "adversary." Thirty-five times he is called "the devil" (Gk., *diabolos*, "slanderer"). He is called "that old serpent" and "the great dragon" (Rev. 12:9), "a roaring lion" (1 Pet. 5:8), "the evil one" (1 John 2:13, NASB*), "Abaddon" and "Apollyon" (Rev. 9:11), "tempter" (Matt. 4:3), "accuser" (Rev. 12:10), and "the spirit that now worketh in the sons of disobedience" (Eph. 2:2).

4. His character

In John 8:44, our Lord describes the devil as a murderer and a liar. He works overtly and covertly with doctrines of devils and seducing spirits. He is a sinner (1 John 3:8), a perverter (1 Tim. 4:1-3), and an imitator (2 Cor. 11:13-15). He is a formidable enemy.

5. His methods

Lucifer and his vast host of demon beings have been around for centuries since they fell. They are clever and cunning. Ephesians 6:11 says that they operate with the wiles of the devil. The Greek word for "wiles" is *methodia*, which means "methods." The same word is used in Ephesians 4:14 and translated as "cunning craftiness." The entire verse says, "That we henceforth be no more children, tossed to and fro, and carried about with every wind of doctrine, by the sleight of men, and cunning craftiness, by which they lie in wait to deceive." The wiles of the devil are lies, false doctrines, false religions,

*New American Standard Bible.

and false teachings. Satan is a liar and the father of lies (John 8:44).

a) Deceptions

Satan is a deceiver. His whole system deceives subtly, supernaturally, cleverly, and powerfully. He has deceived mankind with false religious systems. It is incredible how sophisticated some of them are. I read a report on holistic healing (Brooks Alexander, "Holistic Health from the Inside," *SCP Journal*, August 1978) that proves to me that holistic healing is nothing but a network of occultic demonism. The entire system, ancient and modern, has a most incredible complex demonic origin that could never have been conceived by a human mind. It is so subtle that it has fooled even the most erudite of men in many cultures throughout history.

Satan is clever. He disguises himself as an angel of light (2 Cor. 11:14). In the Old Testament Satan deceived Israel into worshiping idols and turning their backs on the true God. In the New Testament he deceived Israel into murdering their Messiah. And in the future he will deceive Israel into thinking the Antichrist is Christ. He is a deceiver.

b) Lies

Satan specializes in lies, heresies, and false doctrine. He will lie about everything, whether simple or sophisticated. I get upset over false doctrines and cults. False doctrine denies the truth of the Word of God. It manifests itself in the women's liberation movement, which denies God's order for the family. It also manifests itself in homosexuality, in the new morality, and in the old-line religions of the world. Such doctrines are from Satan—they are the wiles of the devil.

(1) To men

Satan moves into the world and prevents God's Word from reaching the hearts of men. He snatches the Word from them (Luke 8:12). He twists and perverts it. He has men in pulpits who deny the authority of Scripture, the deity of Christ, salvation by grace, the second coming, judgment, and sin. He presents a life-style that damns men. He is involved in politics—in governments and nations as well as individual lives.

(2) To Christians

Satan tries to create doubt in the minds of believers, just as he did in Eve's (Gen. 3:1-5), and as he has in God's people throughout history. He persecutes them (Rev. 2:10), hinders their service (1 Thess. 2:18), and infiltrates the church with his tares (Matt. 13:24-30, 36-43). He tempts believers to be self-reliant, to doubt, to lie, and be immoral, worldly, prideful, and discouraged. Many people think that the longer you're a Christian and the more mature you become, the easier life will be. That's not true because the more you know, the more subtle the temptations become.

B. Satan's Men (v. 12)

1. His dupes (v. 12a)

"For we wrestle not against flesh and blood."

Our enemy is not the world system, although we may be persecuted by it someday, just like Jesus was. (In John 15:20 Jesus says, "If they have persecuted me, they will also persecute you.") Don't be surprised; the real enemy is not flesh and blood.

2. His demons (v. 12b)

"But against principalities, against powers, against the rulers of the darkness of this world, against spiritual wickedness in high places."

Those are all terms that describe demons. The demon empire is the real enemy. The word "wrestle" does not refer to an athletic game. When wrestlers went into the ring in Roman times, each one would attempt to get his hands around his opponent's neck in a stranglehold. He then would try to press the opponent's shoulders and head to the ground. If a wrestler's head was pressed to the ground, he was put to death. But if only his shoulders touched, he lived to fight again. Satan wrestles with us through his demons, and it is a life-and-death struggle. Demons know the Bible. They know there is a bottomless pit—an eternal place created for them. And they will do everything they can to get a stranglehold on the things of

God to change that. So our warfare is not on a human level. It is anything but sport.

Beware the "Astral Pigpen"

Satan is so clever, he has people delving into things pertaining to demons. John Weldon, a cult researcher, sent me a report that was later made into a book. An excerpt from it says: "God did not make us in such a way that we can function either safely or effectively in [a demonic] environment, even if it were neutral, which it clearly is not. Who knows what demons can do in their own environment or what interrelationships exist, or can be manufactured between their world and ours? We were not made to fly around in astral realms. Granted the existence of the demonic, one is playing in an astral pig pen, filled with evil, cunning, and hostility.

"We were not made with the intellectual capacities to separate the good (or neutral) from the evil, or the true from the false, etc., in the occult realm or teachings. For example, the prophet Daniel was a brilliant, wise, and godly young man. However, even he had to be given additional special wisdom from God to be able to have discernment in occult matters (Daniel 1:17-20). . . . Thus involvement in the occult will always produce faulty conclusions because man, being a fallen creature, does not have the necessary equipment or abilities to sort out such matters" (*Occult Shock and Psychic Forces* [San Diego: Master Books, 1980], p. 151). He's right. All you need to do is report to the Commander. Put your armor on. Don't get involved in a dominion you can't comprehend.

IV. THE BATTLE (v. 13)

An understanding of the battle is important. It isn't easy to live the Christian life. Yet the only things that matter in life—the only things that taste sweet—are the things you work hard to get. That's where you'll see victory. The greatest joy is to know that you have overcome Satan.

Satan and his demons are all around. I just put my armor on and report to the Commander. I don't care how many demons may attack me; I don't care if Satan himself stands against me because greater is He who is in me than he who is in the world (1 John 4:4). I have a resource in Christ to deal with the demonic domain. Demons will try to stop what God is doing. But they cannot succeed as long as we are faithful to put our confidence in God—not in ourselves—keep our armor on, and live a righteous life. If all hell were to come against us, it would be impotent even if we had only the "little strength" of the church in Philadelphia (Rev. 3:8).

V. THE VICTORY (v. 13)

"Wherefore, take unto you the whole armor of God, that ye may be able to withstand in the evil day, and having done all, to stand."

You can stand in victory if your armor is on and your confidence is in the Lord. Don't get caught with your armor off. You say, "When is the evil day?" Today, yesterday, tomorrow—any day is the evil day as long as evil reigns in the world and as long as Satan is "the prince of the power of the air" (Eph. 2:2). But when you report to the Commander, the victory is yours. Resist the devil and he will flee from you (James 4:7). Isaac Watts asked, "Am I a soldier of the cross?" in the hymn of the same name. But that was the wrong question. We're all soldiers of the cross. The real question is: What kind of a soldier am I? Do I win or lose? There is no reason to know anything but victory. With victory comes joy, happiness, contentment, and peace.

Focusing on the Facts

1. Explain the position of the believer before God (see p. 24).
2. In what ways do a car and a map illustrate the believer's position and practice (see p. 25)?
3. What word best describes the Christian life? Why (see p. 26)?
4. To what degree was Christ attacked as He came closer to accomplishing His goals? Why is that important (see p. 26)?
5. What happens the longer you fight the battle (see pp. 26-27)?
6. In what two realms does the Christian's enemy fight (see pp. 27-28)?
7. What must a Christian do before he enters the battle (see p. 28)?
8. What kind of strength does the believer have available to him (see p. 28)?
9. As a Christian, you were in Christ when He defeated Satan at the cross. As a result of that, what did you do to Satan (see p. 29)?
10. What two things must a Christian do to win the battles in his life (see p. 30)?
11. Describe the power that the Christian has been given through Christ (see p. 30).
12. When is the power of God most available to the Christian (2 Cor. 12:9-10; see p. 31)?

13. Explain how your approach to our battle with Satan should be like that of a guard to the opposing army (see pp. 31-32).
14. According to Ephesians 6:11, what must the believer do with the armor of God? Why is that important (see p. 32)?
15. The Bible doesn't instruct believers to attack the enemy; however, what does it tell them to do (James 4:7; see p. 33)?
16. Describe the background of Satan (see p. 33).
17. Name some of the things that Satan does to fight God (see p. 33).
18. Name the various titles that apply to Satan (see p. 34).
19. Describe the various methods Satan uses to do battle with believers (see p. 34).
20. Describe Satan's approach to unsaved men. Describe his approach to believers (see pp. 35-36).

Pondering the Principles

1. Read through Ephesians 1-3. Based on your reading, write out in your own words what it means to be a believer. Meditate on the reality of your salvation. Take this opportunity to draw near to God in prayer. Thank Him for all He has done for you.
2. Read 1 Corinthians 10:12-13. What happens to you when you become self-confident and stop depending on God? As a soldier of Christ, do you try to fight the battles on your own or do you report the enemy to God? Give an example of a time when you have done one or the other. Why should you allow God to fight the battle instead of doing it yourself? Commit the battle to God and prepare to follow His leadership.
3. Read 2 Corinthians 2:11. According to that verse, what did Paul know about Satan? Can you say the same thing about yourself? Review the section on Satan (see pp. 33–37). Make a list of every biblical reference that refers to the deceptions, lies, and temptations of Satan. Be sure to study those passages so you will not be ignorant of his schemes.

3
The Believer's Warfare—Part 2

Outline

Introduction
A. The Reality of the Battle
B. The Response to the Battle
   1. Indifference
   2. Investment
C. The Recognition of the Battle

Review
 I. The Preparation
   A. Our Strength in Christ
   B. Our Victory in Christ
   C. Our Power in Christ
      1. Its availability

Lesson
      2. Its appropriation
         a) The divine paradox
         b) The decisive choice
      3. Its assurance
         a) John 10:29
         b) Psalm 91:1-2, 4-7
         c) Psalm 34:7
 II. The Armor (Review)
III. The Enemy (Review)
   A. Satan Himself (Review)
   B. Satan's Men
      1. His dupes
      2. His demons
         a) The organization of holy angels
         b) The organization of fallen angels
            (1) "Principalities" and "powers"
            (2) "The rulers of the darkness of this world"
            (3) "Spiritual wickedness in high places"

Introduction

A. The Reality of the Battle

As Paul closes his letter to the Ephesians, he speaks of the great struggle that lies before every believer. The world is a battleground. In fact, the whole universe is at war. There is a war between God and Satan that is recorded in Scripture in many places. Perhaps it is no more clearly seen than in Job 1-2, where God and Satan are in verbal conflict. The conflict between God and Satan appears on other levels: between holy and evil angels and between good and evil men. The warfare began when man fell and the curse entered the earth (Gen. 3:14-19). The Christian life is a battle—a wrestling match, as Paul calls it in Ephesians 6:12. As believers, we exist in a life-and-death struggle.

B. The Response to the Battle

    1. Indifference

I believe it is easy for us to lose a proper perspective about Christianity. It is easy to be proud of your theology when everything is going well. It is easy to forget that a war is going on when your world is beautiful and glorious. You forget that there are millions of souls in the world who are in the grasp of Satan. You forget that Satan is doing subtle things to debilitate you, whether it's lethargy, indolence, indifference, or stagnation. I fear that when I preach about the warfare, everyone wonders what I'm talking about. There are many people who don't even realize what is going on. If you don't know there is a war going on, then you're not a good soldier because you're not fighting.

Getting Off the Bench

When I was young man playing football, the one thing I couldn't stand was sitting on the bench. During my first year in college, I received a severe injury in my first game. The coach decided to leave me on the bench after that because he was afraid I would reinjure myself. One day I said to him, "There is one thing I really hate and that's sitting on the bench. There's a guy playing a position I'm supposed to be backing up, but I know I can do a better job than he can." So the coach said, "Do you want to prove it?" I said, "Yeah, let us go head-to-head and see who wins." One night after practice, he turned the headlights of his car on the field. He then drew a white line on the ground and said, "I'm going to give you forty-five minutes to go head-to-head. When I blow the whistle, you hit each other. We'll see who drives the other one across the white line the most times." That's the way it is in football—if you're going to prove yourself, it's going to be a little tough. So we went at it for forty-five minutes, and it was rough because we both wanted that position. As it turned out, I prevailed. I didn't always prevail, but that time I got the position. The story reminds me that I don't like to sit on the bench. I want to be where the action is, just like the apostle Paul. In 1 Corinthians 16:8-9 he says that he had to stay in Ephesus because there were many adversaries.

Many Christians don't know there is a battle because they don't ever go where the battle is being fought. Instead they hole up in their sanctified environment. I think many are lulled into thinking that the war doesn't exist. Meanwhile, Satan is gaining victory in their lives because of their indifference and lethargy. The greatest tragedy that could ever happen to any church would be for the people to enjoy the fellowship but be indifferent about the battle.

2. Investment

Do you see your life as warfare? Where do you invest your time, money, talent, and energy? If you invest those things in what is passing and mundane, then you don't understand the warfare. A Christian said to me, "The wonderful thing about the Christian life is that basically you can do what you want." I said, "To be very honest with you, I can't remember the last time I did what I wanted." I don't do what I want; I do what I have to do. There are so many things I have to do, I don't even think about what I want to do. But what I really want to do is

43

what I have to do. I am in a war. When I get on an airplane, I would like to be able to read and meditate. But I know what I have to do: Tell the person who is sitting next to me about Christ. I feel compelled, just like the apostle Paul, who said, "For the love of Christ constraineth [me]" (2 Cor. 5:14). We do what we have to do because we are in a battle. You can't let the war pass in front of you without ever fighting in it. This life is warfare and the issue is: What do I do with my life? my dollars? Do I put them in the passing, mundane things of the world or do I put them in things that will make an eternal difference?

The Christian life is a war, but I don't think we understand that. It is easy for us to come to church and enjoy all the entertainment and activities that are provided. But we can do that and never understand how serious life is. I pray to God that the devotion and commitment level of the church will deepen to the point that we will never settle for indifference and complacency. Yet I know there are some who will settle for that.

C. The Recognition of the Battle

In Ephesians 6 Paul wants us to understand that this life is a war. We are in Christ and have all spiritual blessings in the supernatural realm. We have direction for living the Christian life and the fullness of the Spirit of God. We are drowning in the love of God. And we have power to do beyond what we could ask or think. But even though we have all those things, we still must remember that it won't be easy. This life is war. Every child of God is a soldier. We all have been drafted, and there are no deferments. If you don't know there is a war, you just lost the battle.

We have so much in Christ and in the Word of God to give us direction. We have the indwelling Holy Spirit. Yet we can't stand on our own confidence. We can't be smug about all we do have because 1 Corinthians 10:12 says, "Let him that thinketh he standeth take heed lest he fall." We have to recognize that we're in a war. Where do we turn for our resource in this war? In the hymn "Stand Up, Stand Up for Jesus," nineteenth-century hymnwriter George Duffield, Jr., said, "The arm of flesh will fail you—ye dare not trust your own." In the hymn "Awake, Our Souls," Isaac Watts wrote,

From Thee, the ever-flowing spring,
Our souls shall drink a fresh supply:

44

While such as trust their native strength
Shall melt away, and droop, and die.

We can't trust ourselves.

Review

I. THE PREPARATION (v. 10; see p. 28)

   A. Our Strength in Christ (see p. 28)

   B. Our Victory in Christ (see p. 29)

   C. Our Power in Christ (see pp. 29-30)

      1. Its availability (see p. 30)

Lesson

      2. Its appropriation

         a) The divine paradox

God is our strength. He is our resource. We must know that divine energy gives us victory. But Ephesians 6 indicates that we have a part in the battle: "Put on the whole armor of God, that ye may be able to stand against the wiles of the devil" (v. 11). That is the divine paradox: The strength is God's, but the commitment must be ours. The same kind of paradox is seen in salvation: We are saved because we are chosen by God, yet we must believe through faith. The paradox is seen in the Christian life: The apostle Paul said, "I am crucified with Christ: nevertheless I live; yet not I, but Christ liveth in me" (Gal. 2:20). This is my life, yet Christ lives in me. This divine paradox is seen in the revelation of God's Word to man: the book of Ephesians is written by Paul, but only through the inspiration of the Holy Spirit. You were saved by God's sovereignty and grace alone, yet you committed yourself to Christ. You must live the Christian life with diligence and commitment, yet that is possible only through God's power. So we see that we are strong in the Lord and the power of His might, yet we must appropriate the resources. Oliver

Cromwell displayed great theology when he said, "Trust in God and keep your powder dry."

Can You Punch?

When I was little, my father and I watched a boxing match on television. The fighter was standing in his corner, going through a ritual of kicking his feet, putting rosin on his shoes, and then kneeling and crossing himself. I said to my dad, "Does that help?" He said, "It does if he can punch. If he can't punch, it won't do a bit of good." The same kind of thing is true of the Christian life. The strength and power is God's, but we have to put the armor on.

b) The decisive choice

The Christian life is a question of availability and appropriation. Know three things: First, it's a war; second, the power to win is available; and third, you have to appropriate that power. You can choose to be impotent and fruitless, even though residing in you is the power to do beyond what you can even ask or think (Eph. 3:20). You could be lethargic, indifferent, and cold, drifting in and out of church, and still be in heaven for all eternity by the immeasurable grace of God. But if you choose to live that way, you will forfeit the blessing God has for you in this life. And you will fail to glorify God to the extent that you should. You can turn your back on all the available power, blunt the energy of the Spirit of God, and say no to the incomprehensible work that God wants to do through you if you so choose.

God used an accident to turn my life around. There was one thing I asked the Lord at that time: "Lord, if You want me in the ministry, I don't want to be run-of-the-mill. I want to have Your power in my life if I'm going to give my life to this end." This answer has come back all through the years: "The power is available, John. Put your armor on!"

It is senseless for a Christian to live his life in a listless manner, filling himself with the things of the world when the power of the God of the universe is available. The Christian life is a battle. Our enemy is formidable. You can't see him, touch him, or outwit him because he is an enemy of the supernatural realm. There are perhaps millions of demons

46

making up a satanic system that's beyond our comprehension. There is no way your human intellect can deal with that system. But know this: God's power is available. If you put on your armor, the entire evil system is impotent against you. What an incredible truth! God is our strength, but His strength can be appropriated only by obedience.

3. Its assurance

If you're a Christian, you're secure in God's power because His power is enough to hold you.

a) John 10:29—Jesus indicates how secure His sheep are when He says, "My Father, who gave them to me, is greater than all, and no man is able to pluck them out of my Father's hand." People point out that the verse only says, "no man." But that's not true. The Greek text says *oudeis dunatai* which means, "no one has the power." If I am a believer in the Father's hand, no being has the power to pluck me from Him. The Greek word for "pluck" is *harpazein*, which means "to snatch." No one can snatch me out of His hand. The same word is used in Matthew 13:19: "When any one heareth the word of the kingdom, and understandeth it not, then cometh the wicked one, and catcheth away that which was sown in his heart." Satan is a snatcher. But no one can snatch you away from the Father's hand, because He is greater than all. Ultimately we win because there is no power to overcome us.

b) Psalm 91:1-2, 4-7—"He who dwelleth in the secret place of the Most High shall abide under the shadow of the Almighty" (v. 1). What security there is in the secret place of the Most High! We abide in a place that is so secret, no one can take us from there because they don't even know where it is. The psalmist continues, "I will say of the Lord, He is my refuge and my fortress, my God; in him will I trust. . . . He shall cover thee with his feathers, and under his wings shalt thou trust; his truth shall be thy shield and buckler. Thou shalt not be afraid for the terror by night, nor for the arrow that flieth by day, nor for the pestilence that walketh in darkness, nor for the destruction that wasteth at noonday. A thousand shall fall at thy side, and ten thousand at thy right hand, but it shall not come near thee" (vv. 2, 4-7). What a tremendous promise!

c) Psalm 34:7—"The angel of the Lord encampeth round about those who fear him."

As far as the war is concerned, we can't lose because God is greater than all. His power is beyond all. But we can lose the skirmishes. Second Corinthians 2:11 indicates that our sin can give Satan an advantage. It doesn't have to be a big sin either, because it is the little foxes that spoil the vines (Song of Sol. 2:15). The little sin gives Satan a foothold. From that foothold he gains entrance for his demonic efforts. We won't hold the war. No being has the power to snatch us out of the Father's hand. Satan tries to, but he can't overpower God. If Satan is a strong man, then God is a stronger one. Ultimately we win the war, but sadly we keep losing battles because we're not willing to put on the armor of God.

II. THE ARMOR (v. 11a; see p. 32)

III. THE ENEMY (vv. 11b-12; see p. 33)

A. Satan Himself (v. 11a; see p. 33)

B. Satan's Men (v. 12)

1. His dupes (v. 12a)

Ephesians 6:12 says, "For we wrestle not against flesh and blood." Man is not our enemy. That's one good reason we shouldn't hate men. That's the reason Jesus hated sin and loved sinners. The sinner is not the enemy; it's the one behind the sinner who is the real enemy. Jesus weeps for sinners because they are duped: "The god of this age hath blinded the minds of them who believe not, lest the light of the glorious gospel of Christ, who is the image of God, should shine unto them" (2 Cor. 4:4). You should have pity on sinners because they have been duped by Satan. If you're going to hate anyone, hate him and his forces. He is the enemy. Don't be so foolish to think that if you've outwitted man, you've accomplished the victory. Men are not the enemy. We are men ourselves, so we can cope with other men. Our enemy is not human. Paul is making the point that we cannot fight this battle on our own.

2. His demons (v. 12*b*)

As human beings, we are fighting against a superhuman force. Satan is not a solitary enemy; he has a force of demon beings so vast that they are beyond our ability to number. How does Paul define them? Verse 12 says we are fighting "against principalities, against powers, against the rulers of the darkness of this world, against spiritual wickedness in high places." The use of the word "against" separates each of the categories of demon beings. Paul is saying that we are fighting a superhuman foe that is highly organized.

a) The organization of holy angels

God organized the angels.

He created all angels at one time. (Angels do not procreate, so they had to be created at one point in the past.) They all have existed since that time.

They were created differently from each other, just like people. There are different kinds of angels. For example, the Bible talks about archangels (1 Thess. 4:16), cherubim (Gen. 3:24), and seraphim (Isa. 6:2-6). Ephesians 1:21 talks about principalities, powers, thrones, dominions, and mights. God has organized an impressive angelic force.

They all have different functions. Daniel 10:10-21 gives some insight into those functions. God gives orders to archangels, who then disseminate those orders to the host of angels, who then carry them out. In Daniel's case, an angel came to assist him. But while he was coming, he was confronted in the heavens by a demon who held him from accomplishing his purpose. God then dispatched Michael, the archangel, to fight the demon and send the angel on his way. One angel apparently has greater resources in dealing with the foe than another, so there are distinctions among angelic beings.

b) The organization of fallen angels

There are also distinctions among demons.

(1) "Principalities" and "powers"

These demons have high ranks in the satanic hierarchy.

(2) "The rulers of the darkness of this world"

Verse 12 should be translated, "The world rulers of this darkness." These demons have infiltrated the political structure of the world. The word "darkness" refers to hell—the dominion of Satan. Colossians 1:13 says that when you were saved, you were delivered out of the "power of darkness," where there is weeping and gnashing of teeth (Matt. 8:12). In Revelation 9:2-3 out of the darkness of the pit will come filthy, vile locusts that will overrun the earth. Darkness is synonymous with the dominion of demons and the abode of Satan. From this darkness come many world rulers. I believe that demon forces are ruling the world from behind the scenes.

Demonic Conspiracies

People often ask me if I believe there is a worldwide conspiracy. People have called it all kinds of things. Some talk about ancient writings of the Egyptians. Some use the phrase "the Illuminati." Some think there is a conspiracy in America because a pyramid and a Cyclopean eye, which is an occultic symbol, appear on the dollar bill. I'm not too sure those people know what they're talking about. I don't know if their sources of information are correct. But aside from all the peripheral things, there is absolutely no doubt in my mind that there is a global conspiracy involving demons in high places accomplishing their own ends. I am sure that demons are behind the systems of the world. The Old Testament says that the gods of the nations are idols [demons] [Ps. 96:5; cf. 1 Cor. 10:19-20). There is no question in my mind that demons were behind Hitler. I also believe that demons were very active in other world rulers such as Napoleon and Alexander the Great. So there are not only principalities and powers (certain kinds of high ranking demons), but there are also world rulers who have been prey to demonic influence.

I believe the world is Satan's (1 John 5:19). He is "the prince of this world" (John 12:31). He has infiltrated the world with a network of demonic world rulers. In some places that is overt, such as in the case of Idi Amin. But in other places it is covert, such as the demonic forces that are functioning in our own country pushing godless, humanistic, atheistic ends. There is no doubt about the existence of a demonic network. The culmination of the world system is detailed in Revelation 18. The system is known as Babylon and will be destroyed when the Lord Jesus returns to set up His kingdom.

I remember talking to a young man who had come out of the occult. He had reached a high level in what was called *The Mark Age Society*. He had access to some amazing information. At one point he was taught how the demon network functioned. He was given the names of certain demons that were involved in the United Nations, and certain demons that were in various continents and countries. He told me things that were beyond my comprehension. There is no doubt that demonic conspiracy is a biblical reality.

We are in a war that is very sophisticated. There are high ranking and powerful demons who are principalities and powers, and there are other demons who occupy places of world leadership, literally indwelling world leaders.

(3) "Spiritual wickedness in high places"

IV. THE BATTLE (v. 13)

The battle lines are drawn. We fight against an incredible force that we can't see, touch, or outwit. This enemy is deceptive, powerful, and supernatural. That's where the battle lies. The sooner you realize that, the better off you will be. If you don't know there is a battle going on, you have probably lost a few.

A. The Stance of the Believer

What is our part in the warfare? Ephesians 6:13 begins with the word "wherefore." That's an important word. Since our strength is in the Lord, since we have all the available armor, and since the enemy is strong and powerful, Paul says, "Wherefore, take unto you the whole armor of God." You had better put the armor on if the war is as serious as verses 10-12 indicate it is. You can't be indifferent. You can't lose if you put on your armor.

Verse 13 says, "That ye may be able to withstand in the evil day." You say, "When is the evil day?" Today is the evil day. Tomorrow will be the evil day. Everyday has been the evil

51

day since Satan usurped the throne of the world. And it will continue to be the evil day until he is cast into the bottomless pit. Paul concludes verse 13 by saying, "And having done all, to stand." When the shock of battle is over and the dust settles, you should still be standing.

They're Not All Standing

When I was in Scotland, a man approached me in Frazerborough. He wore a backward collar as do many ministers in the Church of Scotland. He had been a minister for many years. He asked me, "Is your father named Jack MacArthur?" I said, "Yes." He said, "Your father came to Ireland at least thirty years ago with two other men to hold a revival in Belfast and all around Ireland. I went to hear your father speak, and at that meeting I received Jesus Christ and dedicated my life to the ministry. I am a pastor because the Lord used your father to minister to me. I wondered if you would tell him that when you see him?" I told him I would. Then he asked, "Where is your father now?" I told him he was pastoring, ministering, and teaching the Word like he always had. He asked, "Is he still faithful to the Word?" I said, "Yes, he is still faithful—still standing." He said, "Good. What happened to the other men?" I said, "One became an apostate; he denied the faith, the truth, and the Word of God. The other man died an alcoholic." Three men went to Ireland thirty years ago and ministered to many people. But thirty years later in the battle, when the dust cleared, they all weren't standing.

I received a letter from a lady who said, "I've come to Grace Church for several years and have been involved in ministry. But I'm leaving because I've decided to marry a non-Christian." She isn't standing anymore.

In 1 Corinthians 9:19-27 Paul says he was willing to preach, fight, and run to win the race for the cause of Jesus Christ. But deep down in his heart he had one gnawing fear: that he might become a "castaway" (v. 27). There are many people who have pastored a church, taught a class, led a Bible study, or led people to Jesus Christ. But when the battle got hot and the smoke cleared, they weren't standing. Do you know why? They didn't have the armor on—or they weren't saved. I've heard people in other churches say, "Why did such terrible things happen in our pastor's life?" He didn't have his armor on—he didn't realize how strong the foe was. But

1. The call

We don't chase the devil. The Bible doesn't instruct us to
find the devil and send him to the pit. It tells us to stand
when demons approach us. The Greek word for "stand"
used in Ephesians 6:13 is the same word used in

a) James 4:7— "Resist the devil, and he will flee from
you."

b) 1 Peter 5:8-9—"The devil, like a roaring lion walketh
about, seeking whom he may devour; whom resist
steadfast in the faith."

We're called to stand and resist. Satan will be constantly attacking you if you are living for God. You
don't have to find him; just stand against him with
the armor on.

2. The fall

Many of you know so much and have so much of the
truth of God. Yet if you don't live the kind of life God
wants you to live, and if you're not equipped for the
battle because you aren't appropriating the resources He
has provided, you're going to fall. It will be a terrible
collapse, and the world will gloat over your failures.

You can forfeit your reward. Second John 8 says, "Look
to yourselves, that we lose not those things which we
have wrought, but that we receive a full reward." You
can receive a reward in heaven to place at the feet of Jesus
Christ, but lose it by falling in this life. When I look at all
that God has given me—a godly heritage, a good education, my ministry, a blessed group of friends who stand
by me in prayer, and fruit beyond anything I could ever
imagine—I'm reminded that those things have been
given by the grace of God. If I were to stumble and fall, I
would forfeit them all. I would be a loser in this life. I
would still be saved, because no man can snatch me out
of the Father's hand, but I would forfeit the blessing, the
fruitfulness, and the reward.

B. The Security of the Believer

1. Dressed in armor

If you're going to stand, you must have the armor on.
Ephesians 6:13-17 describes the armor this way: "Where-

53

fore, take unto you the whole armor of God, that ye may be able to withstand in the evil day, and having done all, to stand. Stand, therefore, having your loins girded about with truth, and having on the breastplate of righteousness, and your feet shod with the preparation of the gospel of peace; above all, taking the shield of faith, with which ye shall be able to quench all the fiery darts of the wicked. And take the helmet of salvation, and the sword of the Spirit, which is the word of God." The more we stand for Christ in the world, the hotter the battle will become, yet we will be glad because God will be glorified even more. We ought to be ready.

2. Dependent on God

Verse 10 tells us that the Lord has the strength; verse 11 tells us to put the armor on because verse 12 says the enemy is strong. Verses 13-17 define the armor. But when we are prepared for the battle, verse 18 says we are to be "praying always." Why? Because even when we are equipped, we are dependent on God. We must covenant to pray for each other. Verse 18 says, "Praying always with all prayer and supplication in the Spirit, and watching thereunto with all perseverance and supplication for all saints." Are you praying for each other in the battle? When we get together for a prayer meeting, we often pray about someone's medical problem. Instead of praying that God would repair bodies, I think we ought to pray more that God would give strength to spirits and souls. That's what our prayer life ought to be focused on. Do you pray for your children to win the battle? Do you pray for your wife to win the battle? Do you pray that she will put on her armor? Do you pray for your husband? Instead of nagging each other, why don't you pray for each other? If we would begin a network of prayer for each other, praying that we would stand firm in the strength of God, I believe God will hear and answer our prayer.

V. THE VICTORY (v. 13)

If we are willing to fight the battle the way God wants it fought and pay the price of victory, I think God will give us ecstasy beyond anything we have ever known. The greatest joys come from the greatest victories. There are so many people who don't understand that this life is a war with many battles. You only have one life. When the last shot is fired, your life will be in the record book. I ask God to give us His strength to win.

Focusing on the Facts

1. Describe the different levels that the conflict between God and Satan can reach (see p. 42).
2. When is a Christian most likely to forget that he is in a war (see p. 42)?
3. What lulls Christians into thinking that the warfare doesn't exist (see p. 43)?
4. Explain the divine paradox about the resources available to the Christian for fighting the war. Name some of the other paradoxes that are seen in the Christian life (see p. 45).
5. What decisive choice must a Christian make if he is to be successful in the battle (see pp. 46-47)?
6. What is the only way a Christian can appropriate God's strength (see pp. 46-48)?
7. How secure is a Christian's salvation? Support your answer with Scripture (see p. 48).
8. How does a Christian give Satan an advantage over him (2 Cor. 2:11; see p. 48)?
9. Why should we love sinners (2 Cor. 4:4; see pp. 48-49)?
10. Who is our enemy besides Satan (Eph. 6:12; see p. 49)?
11. List the various categories of angels (see pp. 49-50).
12. Describe the rulers of the darkness of this world (Eph. 6:12; see p. 50).
13. When is the evil day? What must a Christian do to withstand that day (Eph. 6:13; see p. 51)?
14. According to 1 Corinthians 9:27, what was Paul's one gnawing fear (see p. 52)?
15. When the devil approaches you, what should you do (James 4:7; 1 Pet. 5:8-9; see p. 53)?
16. How can a Christian forfeit his reward (2 John 8; see p. 53)?
17. According to Ephesians 6:18, what must the Christian do after he has put on his armor? Why (see p. 54)?

Pondering the Principles

1. Examine your life. Do you see yourself in constant warfare with Satan? Do you basically do what you want or are you compelled by God to do what He wants you to do? Most of you probably fall somewhere between those two extremes. If that is the case, which extreme are you closer to? If your life is spent mostly in

fulfilling your own desires, then you're not fighting in the war. God wants you to be a soldier in His army, but that requires a commitment. Are you willing to make it? Memorize 2 Timothy 2:4: "No soldier in active service entangles himself in the affairs of everyday life, so that he may please the one who enlisted him as a soldier" (NASB).

2. How often do you find yourself hating someone or being bitter toward someone who has wronged you? Once a month? Once a week? Once a day? We quite often treat our fellow man—and even fellow Christians—as if they were our worst enemies. But who is our real enemy according to Ephesians 6:12? According to 2 Corinthians 4:4, what has the real enemy done to those we often treat as the real enemy? How should we treat our fellow man? Read Ephesians 4:31-32. Begin to follow Paul's exhortation today.

3. Read Ephesians 6:18-20. If we are to be successful in our battles with the enemy, we need to pray always. But whom are we to pray for? Do you pray for members of your family? Do you pray for your friends? We all need help in the battle. Today, set aside a specific portion of your prayer time to ask God to strengthen your family and friends in their battles with the evil one. Be faithful to do so every day.

4
The Believer's Armor—Part 1

Outline

Introduction
A. The Approach of the Believer
  1. His resources
  2. His readiness
B. The Attacks of the Enemy
  1. Undermining God's character and credibility
  2. Making it hard to live the Christian life
    a) Through persecution
    b) Through peer pressure
    c) Through peaceful preoccupation
  3. Confusing the believer with false doctrine
  4. Hindering the believer's service to Christ
    a) 1 Corinthians 16:9
    b) 1 Thessalonians 2:8-9
    c) Acts 20:31
  5. Causing division in the Body of Christ
  6. Urging believers to trust their own resources
  7. Causing the believer to be hypocritical
  8. Making believers worldly
  9. Causing believers to disobey God's Word
C. The Armor of the Believer

Lesson
II. The Belt of Truthfulness
A. The Content of Truth
  1. The inspiration of lies
  2. The imagery of truth
    a) The belt
      (1) Identified
        (*a*) Exodus 12:11
        (*b*) Luke 12:35
      (2) Illustrated

Introduction

We have the wonderful privilege of studying the sixth chapter of Ephesians. I cannot even begin to exhaust the tremendous truths regarding the armor of the Christian. We have learned that the believer is involved in a war. We have seen that this battle is against a formidable enemy—Satan and his host of demons. The committed Christian and Satan are on a collision course. It is inevitable that your life will intersect with the forces of hell as you live for God. The only question is: How will the collision manifest itself? It is not only inevitable, but also constant. The adversary works effectively and powerfully against the child of God.

  A. The Approach of the Believer

      1. His resources

> The Christian possesses tremendous resources. We have received all spiritual blessings in the heavenlies in Christ Jesus (Eph. 1:3). We have been given a place in the Beloved (v. 6). We have been granted forgiveness of sin (v. 7). We have been made sons of God (v. 5). We have been given knowledge, understanding, and wisdom (vv. 17-18). We have been made part of an incredible mystery that was planned before the foundation of the world (v. 4). We have been given the Holy Spirit to seal us with the promise of salvation (v. 13). We have been granted the power to do beyond what we can imagine (3:20). We have been given the capability of expressing that power through the indwelling presence and filling of the Holy Spirit (3:16). We represent the awesome power of God in this world. That very power raised Christ from the dead, set Him at the right hand of the Father, and put all principalities and powers under His feet (1:20-21).

      2. His readiness

As the people of God, we are put in this world to accomplish the goals and purposes that God Himself has designed for His kingdom. It is an effort that is certain to be withstood by the enemy. He is the very enemy who endeavored to withstand God in His own heavens and who withstood man in his innocence in the Garden of Eden. He tried to wipe out the nation of Israel. He tried to stop the birth, life, and resurrection of Jesus Christ. He tries to destroy the church and hinder service rendered by believers. Someday, he will try to force the earth against the power of Christ as He comes to take His rightful place. This formidable foe is pitted against the believer in this age.

A Christian who doesn't recognize the enemy, understand something of his significance, and prepare for battle will be victimized. He will not only lose in this life, but also lose his ability to fulfill what God desires of him. As a result, he will not glorify God. We must be ready for the war; we must be aware of the battles. Those who really study the Bible know this war is serious, but I'm afraid it's not taken as seriously as it ought to be with many of you. God has put it on my heart to reiterate the tremendous importance of this battle and what He is asking of us.

B. The Attacks of the Enemy

Since the believer and Satan are on an absolute and constant collision course, we need to understand how Satan attacks. The Bible verifies that Satan does attack in specific ways. The following are ways that Satan attacks believers. And I have seen them acted out in my life and in the lives of others.

1. Undermining God's character and credibility

Satan desires to undermine God. He wants you to doubt God. He did that in the Garden of Eden when he asked Eve, "Hath God said?" (Gen. 3:1). He then impugned God's motives by saying that God didn't want Adam and Eve to eat from the tree of good and evil because He didn't want them to be like Him. Satan tried to ascribe to God a selfish, ulterior motive. He was saying that they couldn't trust or believe God because He might say one thing but mean something else. The New Testament says that if you don't believe God, you have made Him a liar (1 John 5:10). God tells us He is truth and that Satan is a liar, but Satan tells us he is truth and that God is a liar.

Satan wants you to doubt God—to doubt His Word and His power. And we do quite often. We're tempted to worry and lose control in a difficult situation because we don't really believe God can solve our problems. We question His power. Sometimes we doubt God's grace, mercy, and forgiveness. We sin and become burdened by feelings of anxiety and guilt. There are people who commit suicide because they cannot accept the forgiveness of God. That is nothing but a denial of His promise and His Word. We also frequently doubt God's love. We think God doesn't really love us when bad things happen, such as a husband leaving or children turning out badly. Satan pushes us to doubt the love of God. Satan attacked Peter and caused him to doubt the truth of God (Luke 22:54-62). Jesus warned Peter to be careful because Satan desired to sift him as wheat (Luke 22:31). Satan attacks us by undermining God's character and credibility. As soon as you begin to doubt Him, consider the source that is causing you to do so.

2. Making it hard to live the Christian life

Satan doesn't want your life to be easy; he wants it to be very difficult. I believe he makes this attack in three ways:

   a) Through persecution

   Living the Christian life is hard because some people are antagonistic toward Christians. A man told me that he talked to his brother about his new faith in Christ. As he showed his brother his Bible and began to talk about it, his brother grabbed the Bible and threw it across the room. He told him, "Don't ever push that book on me." That is an illustration of mild persecution. There are many illustrations of severe persecution throughout the history of the church. Persecution may come while you are on the job; it may even come from your friends.

   b) Through peer pressure

   Some people don't want to live for God because they don't want to lose their friends and be thought of as different. They don't want to have to change their relationships because they are comfortable being accepted; they like being liked. They're not ready to take a step in a different direction that could alienate them from their friends. The writer of Hebrews was dealing with that kind of attitude as he addressed members of the Jewish community who were sitting on the fence. They hadn't committed themselves to Christ—although they believed the truth about Him—for fear of what their friends and their family would say. They didn't want to be ostracized. Paul said, "All that will live godly in Christ Jesus shall suffer persecution" (2 Tim. 3:12).

c) Through peaceful preoccupation

There are times when the hardest place to live the Christian life is in the easiest place. In America, being a Christian is acceptable and respectable. The majority are supposedly born-again Christians. Religion is the mood of the hour. Christianity is a good thing. It's easy to be a Christian in America because there's no price to pay. And that's what makes living the Christian life the hardest of all. We might be able to respond correctly when confronted by peer pressure or persecution, but it's tougher to make a stand for Christ when we are readily accepted by people.

Satan endeavors to make it hard to live for Christ.

3. Confusing the believer with false doctrine

I often talk to Christians who don't understand what the Bible means. A man asked me, "What is sanctification? I'm so confused." And he has been a Christian for a long time. The confusion is compounded by different books and teachers. People say, "Why do so many people disagree?" I believe the confusion is partly a ploy of Satan to frustrate Christians. There are people who say, "You can't be dogmatic about the Bible; you have to accept it in general." People have said to me, "Why are you so dogmatic all the time? You can't be that dogmatic about the Bible!" If you study the Bible, it isn't that hard to understand. I'm not the smartest person around; I'm of average intelligence. But I do know how to dig into the Bible to find out what it means. Satan confuses believers by presenting a plethora of interpretations that leave many people baffled. He also confuses believers with false teachers who sow all kinds of wrong doctrine. Many Christians are "tossed to and fro, and carried about with every wind of doctrine" (Eph. 4:14). Many Christians are deceived by false teachers who come "in sheep's clothing, but inwardly they are ravening wolves" (Matt. 7:15).

There are problems in the church today because the doctrines of demons are so rampant. Satan is confusing the church. Many Christian people are sending millions of dollars to the wrong causes. False teaching adds much confusion about what is true in the Bible. Satan tries to undermine God's character, make it hard to live the Christian life, and confuse Christians with false teachers and false doctrines.

4. Hindering the believer's service to Christ

   Satan wants to stop effective service. He wants to stop Grace Church. He wants to stop my ministry, your ministry, and the ministry of anyone who is serving Jesus Christ. Throughout the Old Testament he tried to hinder the prophets of God. He tried to hinder the Lord Jesus Christ. And he tried to hinder the apostle Paul.

   a) 1 Corinthians 16:9—"There are many adversaries."

   b) 1 Thessalonians 2:8-9—"So, being affectionately desirous of you, we were willing to have imparted unto you, not the gospel of God only but also our own souls, because ye were dear unto us. For ye remember, brethren, our labor and travail; for laboring night and day . . . we preached unto you the gospel of God." Christian service is hard work.

   c) Acts 20:31—Paul told the Ephesians elders, "I ceased not to warn everyone night and day with tears." Why? Because it is hard to serve.

   Young men have asked me, "Does it get easier the longer you minister?" No, but the string of victories gets more wonderful. You then have a better history to build your faith upon for the future. But it never gets any easier, because Satan hinders our service.

5. Causing division in the Body of Christ

   Satan works hard to cause division. That's why our Lord said that if you have anything against your brother, be reconciled to him before you come to worship God (Matt. 5:24). First Corinthians 1-3 discusses the problem of division in the church. In Ephesians 4:3 Paul says, "[Endeavor] to keep the unity of the Spirit in the bond of peace." Paul exhorts us in that area because Satan will try to rip us apart by bringing friction into the body of Christ.

6. Urging believers to trust their own resources

This is a subtle effort on the part of Satan. First Chronicles 21 tells the story of David's desire to find out how strong he was. So he counted his soldiers. But God told him that was a terrible sin because his strength was not dependent upon the number of his troops but on God. It's easy for believers to count on what they know. You might say, "I've memorized a book of the Bible. I've mastered some important principles. I've been to seminary. I'm ready and able to handle any problems." But what happens? Your prayer life becomes nonexistent, the depth of your devotion is lost, and you become shallow and theological. There are some people who think that since they go to church all the time, their spiritual life is adequate. It is easy for us to be confident in our own resources and to lean on our own understanding (Prov. 3:5). We depend on our own knowledge, wisdom, insight, and education, but fail to cast ourselves upon the power of God. Isaiah had the right perspective when he said, "Woe is me!" (Isa. 6:5). He knew he had no resource apart from God.

7. Causing the believer to be hypocritical

Satan has populated every church with people who are phony. Christians are capable of being phony. We can mask our spirituality by allowing the world to think we are fine, but we pollute the fellowship in the process. We are so good at masking ourselves that we never deal with the real problem. We never let anyone see what we are really like. We never open up and tell the truth. That means no one can ever wrap their arms around us and help deliver us from our problems. We hide behind respectability. We hide behind our hypocritical spirituality. We are like Ananias and Sapphira, who lied to the Holy Spirit (Acts 5:1-11). Satan has played a game on us. He has told us that it is better to be thought respectable than to actually be respectable. He has told us that it is better to cover up your sin than to face it and deal with it. Satan is subtle. He fills the church with hypocrisy.

8. Making believers worldly

Satan wants to put us into the world's mold. He is so successful at this that the church today has become worldly, affluent, materialistic, and self-indulgent. It has become so much like the world system that it's hard to separate the two. The apostle John says, "Love not the world, neither the things that are in the world. If any man love the world, the love of the Father is not in him. For all that is in the world, the lust of the flesh, and the lust of the eyes, and the pride of life, is not of the Father, but is of the world. And the world passeth away, and the lust of it; but he that doeth the will of God abideth forever" (1 John 2:15-17). John is saying that you have no business having a relationship with the world. The world is passing, but you are eternal. The church is engulfed because Satan constantly pushes us into the world.

9. Causing believers to disobey God's Word

    This attack may be the pinnacle of Satan's schemes. He wants us to act immorally. If God is moral and sets the moral law, then any act against God's law is immoral, whether it is sexual or social. To act immorally is to act against the moral law and the God who established it. Satan wants us to disobey God to gain an advantage.

In summary, these are nine ways that Satan attacks us: He tries to undermine God's character, make it hard to live the Christian life, confuse us with false doctrine, hinder our service, cause division, force us to trust in our own resources, make us play the hypocrite, cause us to become worldly, and make us disobey God. That's how his attack will come.

C. The Armor of the Believer

You say, "How do I deal with Satan's attacks?" The wonderful thing is that all his attacks can be dealt with in one simple way. Ephesians 6:13 says, "Wherefore, take unto you the whole armor of God, that ye may be able to withstand in the evil day, and having done all, to stand." How can you resist all of Satan's complex, subtle attacks? How can you deal with his cunning craftiness and deceitfulness? Simple: Don't concentrate on what he is doing; concentrate on what you are doing. It's not that important to categorize his attacks. It doesn't matter so much that you identify every subtlety. You can't do that anyway. The world is too sophisticated, remote, and superhuman for you to deal with. The only thing that does matter is that you put your armor on. Whenever the battle starts and whatever his attack might be, you will be defensible. It doesn't matter where the enemy comes from, or how subtle his attack is; the only thing that matters is that you're ready for it. The believer who wears his armor will stand, whatever the attack. Be aware of Satan's attacks. The major issue is not how he attacks, but that you are ready. Are you ready? If you have your armor on, you can handle any attack.

I want to look at the first piece of armor. It is found in Ephesians 6:14, which begins, "Stand, therefore." That verse refers us back to verse 13: "Having done all, to stand." Verse 11 says, "That ye may be able to stand." Paul is telling us to stand against the attack of Satan and be victorious when he comes.

Lesson

I. THE BELT OF TRUTHFULNESS (v. 14a)

The Greek word *alētheia* can be translated as "truth as content," "truth as opposed to falsehood," or "truth as the Word of God." It can also be described as an attitude of truthfulness, sincerity, honesty, integrity, or commitment.

A. The Content of Truth

If Satan attacks me, it is incumbent upon me to have the belt of truth. Why?

1. The inspiration of lies

   Satan will attack with his wiles (v. 11). The Greek word for "wiles" is translated "cunning craftiness" in Ephesians 4:14. That verse refers to various kinds of doctrine or teachings. Satan will send teachings that are cunningly deceiving. Those false truths are the wiles of the devil. The only way you can resist the lies of the devil is to have the truth. That is why it is so important for us to continually teach the Word of God.

   Paul says that people will follow doctrines of demons and seducing spirits (1 Tim. 4:1). For example, the Corinthians would go to pagan temples and worship their gods with many rituals and ceremonies. But in 1 Corinthians 10:20 Paul says, "The things which the Gentiles sacrifice, they sacrifice to demons, and not to God." Demons were behind the entire Corinthian religious system. Their worship was demonic. That gives us insight into all false teaching: It comes from Satan. In John 8:44 Jesus said of Satan, "He is a liar, and the father of [lies]." Satan attacks with lies. Since a believer is going to war, he must know the truth.

2. The imagery of truth

a) The belt

(1) Identified

In Paul's day, a Roman soldier wore a tunic. A tunic was a large square piece of material that had holes for the head and arms. It hung low and loose over the body. But if you were going into a battle, you wouldn't want it in the way. A soldier never started on a journey with a loose tunic.

(*a*) Exodus 12:11—When the children of Israel were called by God to leave for the Promised Land, they needed to have their loins girded up. That was a common phrase for someone taking a journey.

(*b*) Luke 12:35—The Lord was talking about His second coming when He said, "Let your loins be girded about, and your lamps burning."

Girding the loins meant gathering up the loose material of the tunic when getting ready to leave. It refers to readiness or preparedness. The belt symbolized preparedness. The Roman soldier wouldn't go into a battle with his tunic flapping in the breeze. If he did, his enemy would pull it over his head—and that would be the end of him. No soldier would fight in a battle with his tunic flapping.

(2) Illustrated

In a football game, the uniforms are usually very tight on the players because they don't want anyone grabbing them. I would get angry when the shirttail of my jersey was flapping in the breeze. I would be running, and someone would grab it and yank me down from behind. Finally, breakaway jerseys were invented. They are worn by many colleges. You might see a player running down the field with half his jersey gone while the opponent will be holding the other half. No player wants his uniform flapping around during the game. The same thing was true in warfare for Roman soldiers. They didn't fight their enemies from bunkers two hundred yards apart; they fought in hand-to-hand combat. They didn't want anything entangling them. In 2 Timothy 2:3-4 the apostle Paul says, "Endure hardness, as a good soldier of Jesus Christ. No man that warreth entangleth himself with the affairs of this life." Paul is saying that you can't fight if you are tangled up in your robe. The affairs of this life have the same effect on the Christian soldier. He must cut the cord with civilian life and make a clean break with the world.

When someone is drafted into the service, he doesn't hear, "Now that we've drafted you, it would certainly be nice if you could wear our uniform. It would also be nice if you would take orders, eat our food, and live in our barracks." You are expected to do that. When you are drafted, you are cut off from your girl friend or wife, home, family, car, and job. Your civilian life is gone. It is a serious thing when someone goes to war. If a man on a journey girded up his loins, you can imagine that a soldier going to war would do the same. He would cinch a belt around his waist. This belt could be made of a sash material, but most likely a soldier's belt would be made out of leather. He would pull the four corners of his tunic up through that leather belt, making it into a kind of mini-tunic. Thus he would have mobility and flexibility without the tunic in his way. That's the imagery that was in the mind of the apostle Paul.

b) The strap

It was also common for a Roman soldier to wear a strap. It connected to the belt in the front, went over the soldier's shoulder, and connected to the belt in the back. He could attach his sword to it. Paul indicates in Ephesians 6:17 that the sword of the Spirit is the Word of God. Taking the imagery further, the sword of the Spirit is attached to the belt of truth, indicating that truth is revealed in the Word. You have the truth in the form of the sword of the Spirit to fight the battle.

Other things attached to the strap were emblems of previous victories. They were decorations that the soldier received for his accomplishments during bat-tle. So all medals were placed on the soldier's strap.

When you wear the belt of truth and draw the sword of the Spirit, you're going to win the battle and receive rewards. The strap became the emblem of accomplishment in battle. The belt and the strap were a fitting combination. Only those with the sword of the Spirit attached to the strap won the medals. They went into battle having already been victorious.

B. The Attitude of Truthfulness

The belt does not refer to the truth itself. The Greek word *alētheia* can be used in the sense of content. But that's not the primary thought Paul had in mind when he made reference to the belt because he dealt with the content of truth in the sword of the Spirit. Paul's main thrust here is the idea of truthfulness. He is using it to refer to attitude, not content. He is saying that when you put your belt on, you reveal an attitude of readiness and commitment. You need to fight without hypocrisy.

Are You Running Your Race in Combat Boots?

Most Christians never put the belt on. They live with little commitment, never displaying an attitude of truthfulness. When a soldier put on his belt, attached the strap, and hooked on his sword, he was saying, "I am ready to fight." I think most Christians lose out because they don't care enough. They would just as soon be uncommitted. Hebrews 12:1 says, "Wherefore, seeing we also are compassed about with so great a cloud of witnesses, let us lay aside every weight, and the sin which doth so easily beset us, and let us run with patience the race that is set before us." Could you imagine someone running in a track meet wearing an over-coat and combat boots? That would be ridiculous! Runners wear so little because they want to be mobile; they want all the flexibility they can get. Yet Christians are trying to run the Christian race wearing combat boots and an overcoat. No wonder they get so tired and never seem to get very far. Five years later they are ten feet from the starting line. Why? Because they have no commitment.

I believe the greatest synonym for truthfulness is commit-ment.

1. Have a heart for the battle

Paul is saying, "You must realize that you are in a war, so get serious! You've got to enter into it without hypocrisy and with the right attitude. You need to have a heart for the battle." Paul was a soldier, willing to endure hardness for the cause of Jesus Christ (2 Tim. 2:3). He was willing to pay the price so he could please the One who chose him to be a soldier (v. 4). Be sure to have a heart for the battle.

2. Live to win

The true Christian loves to win the fight. And he loves the Lord so much, he won't lose because he won't give up. I can't relate to a Christian who is content to be defeated all the time, falling into the temptation of the sins of the flesh and the mind. How can you keep from giving in so easily?

a) Through desire

In 1 Corinthians 9:24 Paul says, "Do you not know that those who run in a race all run, but only one receives the prize? Run in such a way that you may win" (NASB). Paul is saying that if you're going to enter the race, try to win it. Who wants to lose? Paul is talking about desire. When I participated in football, desire was ninety percent of the game. If you want to win badly enough, the victory is there for the taking. My coaches used to say, "If you want victory badly enough, you can get it." Now that was a good thought, but it isn't always true. Sometimes I would play across the line from a guy who was tougher than I was. I may have wanted the victory badly enough, but nothing I did against him would work. I was eating dirt all day. Some of my greatest efforts were against the worst adversaries, yet I still couldn't win. But when it comes to the cause of Christ, if you have the desire, the victory will be yours. Why? Because "greater is he that is in you, than he that is in the world" (1 John 4:4). Victory for the Christian is always available, but the desire has to be there. An athlete runs with a lot of people, but only one gets the prize. If you're going to run, run to win.

May God give people to the church who have that kind of commitment—people who want to win in the Christian life, not so they can stack up their own crowns, but so they can give them to Jesus Christ as their living sacrifice of love, worship, and praise. That's what Paul was looking for—commitment.

b) Through discipline

In 1 Corinthians 9:25 Paul says, "And every man that striveth for the mastery is temperate in all things." An athlete disciplines his life. He is careful about what he eats and how he trains. Paul continues, "Now they do it to obtain a corruptible crown, but we, an incorruptible" (v. 25). Paul is saying that if athletes can work hard to win a corruptible crown, we should have the desire to be victorious in our lives for God's glory. Paul then concludes, "I, therefore, so run, not as uncertainly; so fight I, not as one that beateth the air; but I keep under my body, and bring it into subjection" (vv. 26-27). That is the disciplined life of a winner. That is what God wants from you.

3. Sacrifice your life to God

In the spiritual realm, God has given us the resources we need to win. In Romans 12:1 Paul says, "I beseech you therefore, brethren, by the mercies of God." What are the mercies of God? The first eleven chapters of Romans. God has set us aside from the evil world, redeemed us in Christ, given us the righteousness of Jesus Christ, called us into His family through our faith in Christ, and adopted us as sons. God has given us love, joy, and peace. He has granted to us the tremendous power of the Spirit of God in resurrection life. He has given to us all the resources we need and set us apart for His eternal plan, which is unchangeable. All those wondrous mercies of God have been given to us; therefore Paul says, "Present your bodies a living sacrifice, holy, acceptable unto God, which is your reasonable service. And be not conformed to this world, but be ye transformed by the renewing of your mind, that ye may prove what is that good, and acceptable, and perfect, will of God" (vv. 1-2). First your mind is renewed through the Word. When you have the truth, you then live with commitment, presenting your life as a sacrifice to God.

Most of us haven't the faintest idea of what it is to sacrifice our lives. It might be easier for us to be burned at the stake for Jesus than to try to live for Him sacrificially! Most of us wouldn't mind if our lives were taken; we just want to live on our own while we are alive. But we are to be committed.

4. Abound in knowledge, love, and discernment

Philippians 1:9-10 says, "And this I pray, that your love may abound yet more and more in knowledge and in all judgment; that ye may approve [test] things that are excellent." Paul is saying, "I don't want you to be satisfied with what is good; I want you to be satisfied with what is excellent. I know you have love, knowledge, and discernment, but I want you to have more. Then he says, "That ye may be sincere [committed, truthful] and without offense till the day of Christ" (v. 10). The result of living a committed and truthful life is found in verse 11: "Being filled with the fruits of righteousness, which are by Jesus Christ, unto the glory and praise of God." Do you know why I want you to be committed? It is not for my personal ambition or for your sake but for the glory and praise of God. He will be glorified when you are filled with the fruit of righteousness. You will be filled with that fruit when you approve what is excellent. And you will approve what is excellent when you are genuinely committed to Jesus Christ.

The first piece of the armor of the believer calls for commitment. You're not going to beat Satan on your own. He will come at you in all the nine ways we looked at. But you're not going to know what to do unless you are ready to fight.

Conclusion

The only thing that ultimately matters in this world is the dimension of the spiritual. I'm concerned about many things in our world, but I couldn't care less about most of them unless they relate to the things of God. Spiritual matters are most important. God must be glorified. We need to focus on that.

How badly do you want to win? I've been involved in athletics all my life and seen people who didn't care about winning. That's true with many professional athletes. They can lose the desire because they've made it. They just go through the motions. And if that can happen in the athletic world, it can happen to Christians. Satan wants us to be content with mediocrity and lethargy. You can come to church week after week, go home, and nothing changes. Your attitudes remain the same, your reactions are the same, and your home stays the same. Nothing ever happens because your commitment never changes.

God help you. And God help me if that happens in my life. We must be committed to the fight. That's why the apostle Paul says that the first piece of equipment is the belt of truthfulness. Content is vital, but it's the right attitude he is looking for here.

Let me close with the hymn "Fight the Good Fight with All Thy Might" by John Monsell:

> Fight the good fight with all thy might!
> Christ is thy strength, and Christ thy right;
> Lay hold on life, and it shall be
> Thy joy and crown eternally.
>
> Run the straight race thro' God's good grace,
> Lift up thine eyes, and seek His face;
> Life with its way before us lies,
> Christ is the path, and Christ the prize.
>
> Cast care aside, lean on thy Guide,
> His boundless mercy will provide;
> Trust, and thy trusting soul shall prove
> Christ is its life, and Christ its love.
>
> Faint not nor fear, His arms are near,
> He changeth not, and thou art dear;
> Only believe, and thou shalt see
> That Christ is all in all to thee.

Victory is available. It's ours to the glory of God if we wear the belt of commitment, no matter how sophisticated Satan may be. I pray that might be true in your life.

Focusing on the Facts

1. List some of the things the enemy has tried to accomplish since he first withstood God (see p. 59).
2. What will happen to the Christian who doesn't recognize the enemy and isn't ready for the battle (see p. 59)?
3. What does Satan try to undermine? Explain (see pp. 59-60).
4. How do people make God out to be a liar? Who is the real liar (see p. 59)?
5. What are some of the things a believer has a tendency to doubt about God (see p. 60)?
6. What are three methods Satan uses to make the Christian life difficult to live? Explain each one (see pp. 60-61).
7. Describe some of the ways that Satan tries to confuse believers (see pp. 61-62).

8. Why doesn't ministry become easier the longer you do it (see p. 62)?
9. Why do Christians constantly need to be reminded to preserve the unity of the Spirit (Eph. 4:3; p. 62)?
10. What perspective should a Christian have about himself (Isa. 6:5; see p. 63)?
11. What is the result when Christians mask their true spirituality (see p. 63)?
12. In what ways has the church become like the world around it (see pp. 63-64)?
13. What is any act that goes against God's moral law (see p. 64)?
14. What is the best way for a Christian to defend himself against the attacks of Satan (Eph. 6:13; see pp. 64-65)?
15. Give some definitions for the Greek word *alētheia* (see p. 65).
16. What are the "wiles" of Satan (see p. 65)?
17. What is the source of all false teaching (John 8:44; see p. 65)?
18. During the time of Christ, what did the phrase "gird up the loins" mean (see p. 66)?
19. What was the purpose of the Roman soldier's belt? What was the purpose of his strap (see pp. 66-67)?
20. What was Paul's primary thought when he referred to the belt of truth (see p. 68)?
21. Why are so many Christians not very far along in the Christian race (see p. 68)?
22. Why will a Christian always prevail against the enemy when he has the desire to (1 John 4:4; see pp. 69-70)?
23. List some of the mercies of God (see p. 70).
24. Based on the mercies that God has given to every believer, what are we to do (Rom. 12:1-2; see pp. 70-71)?
25. What is the result of living a committed, truthful, and sincere life (Phil. 1:10; see p. 72)?

Pondering the Principles

1. Review the section that discusses the attacks of the enemy (see pp. 59-60). Give an example of how Satan has attacked you in each of those ways. In each case, did you realize that the attack was from Satan? If not, who did you think was attacking you and why? In those cases that you were sure Satan was the source of the attack, how did you defend yourself? Was your defense successful? Based on this lesson, how would you defend yourself now? What is the one thing you must do to successfully defend yourself against him? Be consistent in your effort.
2. Read 2 Timothy 2:3-4. Do you view yourself as a soldier of Christ?

If you don't see yourself as a soldier, then how do you see yourself? Does your answer indicate that you are still attached to the world? What are the affairs of this world that keep you from being a soldier on active duty in Christ's army? How important are they in comparison to your relationship to Christ? Suppose God gave you this choice: You must either give up the affairs of this life or give up your relationship to Christ. What would you give up? Take this time to ask God to show you how to give up those things that pull at you from the world. Become attached to Christ.

3. Take the following test on your commitment to the Christian life:
    a) Do you have a heart for the battle? Yes or No.
    b) Which of the following statements best describes your dedication to winning in the Christian life:
       (1) I have the desire but not the discipline.
       (2) I have the discipline but not the desire.
       (3) I have the desire and the discipline.
       (4) None of the above.
    c) How often do you sacrifice your life to God?
       (1) Daily.
       (2) Once a week.
       (3) Once a month.
       (4) I'm not sure I even know what it means to sacrifice my life to God.
    d) Is your life characterized by love, knowledge, and discernment?
       (1) I have enough to get by.
       (2) I wish I had more.
       (3) I'm characterized more by hate, ignorance, and foolishness.

What do you think the correct answers should be? When you decide how badly you want to win the battle of the Christian life, you will need not be ashamed to take this test.

5
The Believer's Armor—Part 2

Outline

Introduction
A. Experiencing the Victory
B. Evaluating the Strategy

Review
  I. The Belt of Truthfulness

Lesson
 II. The Breastplate of Righteousness
    A. The Picture
    B. The Priority
    C. The Protection
       1. The vital areas
          a) The heart
             (1) Proverbs 23:7
             (2) Mark 7:21
             (3) Jeremiah 17:9
          b) The bowels
       2. The vicious attack
          a) On the mind
          b) On the emotions
    D. The Possibilities
       1. Self-righteousness
          a) Of the scribes and Pharisees
             (1) Matthew 5:20
             (2) Luke 18:10-14
          b) Of man
             (1) Isaiah 64:6
             (2) Romans 3:10-12, 19, 23
          c) Of the apostle Paul
       2. Imputed righteousness
          a) In Paul's life

Introduction

In the book of Ephesians the apostle Paul has outlined the tremendous resources of the Christian. But he doesn't want us to be overconfident or under the illusion that our resources will make our war with the forces of hell easy. It is true that we have been blessed with all spiritual blessings in the heavenlies (Eph. 1:3). We are able to do exceedingly abundantly above all we can ask or think (3:20). We can be filled with the Spirit of God and all His might (5:18). We may have all those resources, the very truth of God in our hearts, and be doing His good works, but that does not mean the Christian life will be easy. That is why Paul says, "Finally, my brethren, be strong in the Lord, and in the power of his might. Put on the whole armor of God, that ye may be able to stand against the wiles of the devil. For we wrestle not against flesh and blood, but against principalities, against powers, against the rulers of the darkness of this world, against spiritual wickedness in high places. Wherefore, take unto you the whole armor of God, that ye may be able to withstand in the evil day, and having done all, to stand. Stand, therefore, having your loins girded about with truth, and having on the breastplate of righteousness, and your feet shod with the preparation of the gospel of peace; above all, taking the shield of faith, with which ye shall be able to quench all the fiery darts of the wicked. And take the helmet of salvation, and the sword of the Spirit, which is the word of God" (Eph. 6:10-17).

A. Experiencing the Victory

In this passage, the apostle Paul outlines the believer's warfare. The sum of it is that we must put on all the armor if we are to be victorious (vv. 11, 13). This is a critical passage on the Christian life. No matter how adept your theology or how solid your comprehension of Scripture, you are a potential loser. This war is fought and won on a day-to-day basis. Despite having intellectual and spiritual resources, which are founded in the power and presence of the Spirit of God, you can lose the daily battle. Paul reminds us that the Christian life is war. The sooner we learn that, the sooner we will experience the victory God has planned for us.

B. Evaluating the Strategy

Luke 14:31 says, "What king, going to make war against another king, sitteth not down first, and consulteth whether he is able with ten thousand to meet him that cometh against him with twenty thousand?" What king ever entered into a battle without a careful examination of his resources and a development of his strategy? In essence, that is what we're doing in Ephesians 6: Given that we are in a war, we must have a careful evaluation of the strategy and resources available to us to win the war against the enemy. And nothing short of total commitment will win it.

Review

I. THE BELT OF TRUTHFULNESS (v. 14a; see p. 65)

Envisioning a Roman soldier in full battle regalia, Paul says, "Stand, therefore, having your loins girded about with truth [Gk., *alētheia*]" (v. 14). Primarily, Paul had truthfulness in mind, or an attitude of readiness—commitment without hypocrisy. The phrase "having your loins girded" is a Hebrew expression indicating readiness or preparedness. When the Jewish people left the land of Egypt at the time of the Passover, they were instructed to gird up their loins (Ex. 12:11). The apostle Peter was calling for the same thing in a spiritual sense when he said, "Wherefore, gird up the loins of your mind" (1 Pet. 1:13). In other words, "Prepare your mind for the things of God." A Jewish person preparing for a trip wouldn't leave with his garments loose; he would put on a belt and pull his garments through it. He was then ready to move. The same thing was true of a Roman soldier. He would pull his tunic through his belt so his garment wouldn't be in his way when he was in battle. The apostle Paul is telling us that we must be prepared and committed for battle.

A Challenge to Commitment

One thing that happens as a church begins to grow is that more and more people are added to the periphery. It seems as if there is a diminishing of commitment at the extremities. People on the periphery don't feel like a part of the core. They are spectators. It is important for us to constantly challenge people to commitment. The more the church grows, the greater its potential impact, the greater the enemy's resistance, and the greater the need for commitment will be.

General Zonik Shaham is an Israeli with a string of battle credits. He is quite a man, although not a Christian. He has a Zionist orientation: He believes in the sovereignty of the State of Israel and has a high regard for the great tradition and history of his people. He said to me, "I appreciated your sermon last Sunday. I especially appreciated what you said about commitment because that is the whole issue with us. People think Israelis are a super people with a super intellect and strength. They think we win because of that, but we win by commitment." Then he said, "We still use the phrase 'gird up your loins' to mean commitment and preparedness. Let me give you an illustration of that. I have a Jewish friend who lives in the San Fernando Valley. His son desired to live in Israel. After living there for several years, he reached the age where he would have to enter the military or return to the United States. I thought that, like other Americans, he would choose the life of ease and return to America rather than enter the Israeli Army. So I was surprised when he joined the army. I then received a letter from him asking for a private appointment with me. I assumed he would ask me to find him a desk job. He showed up at my office requesting a favor. He told me that his assignment in the army was too easy. Instead, he wanted to be in the finest, most strategic, diligent, and difficult regiment in all the Israeli Army." General Shaham informed him that a frontline, crack regiment of paratroopers had the most precarious duty. They dropped into an area before anyone else. But then he told him that the effort it took to be in that regiment was incredible. The training closed with four days of relentless marching through the desert with full pack to eventually climb up the mountain that leads to Masada. But that's what the man wanted, so he signed up. General Shaham said, "That's why we win—we have people like him who are committed." That is essentially what the apostle Paul is telling us in the concept of the belt of truthfulness.

We are in a war. The world deludes us with the good life, but we are in the middle of a spiritual battle. We will win when we get serious about the battle. I believe there is no limit to what God can do through us, other than our own lack of commitment. I think that's where it has to begin.

Lesson

II. THE BREASTPLATE OF RIGHTEOUSNESS (v. 14*b*)

No Roman soldier in his right mind would ever go into a battle without his breastplate. Even if he could defeat his foe, he might get hit in a vulnerable place by an arrow shot from another enemy. Certainly he had vulnerable areas as he fought in hand-to-hand combat, but if he was protected, many blows wouldn't harm him. So Paul pictures a Roman soldier going into battle. We know he is committed because his loins are girded by his belt and his vital areas are protected by his breastplate.

A. The Picture

Roman soldiers had different kinds of breastplates. Some of them were made out of heavy linen that hung down very low. The linen would be covered with thin slices from the hooves or horns of an animal. Those slices would then be hooked together and hung from the linen. Pieces of metal might also be on the linen. The most familiar type of breastplate was the molded metal chest plate that covered the vital areas of the torso from the base of the neck to the top of the thighs.

B. The Priority

Through the years I've studied the armor of the Christian to see if there's any hierarchy or priority to the individual pieces. But that's very difficult to discern because we are to put on "the whole armor of God." Each piece is specifically designed to accomplish an essential function. That's why we cannot say that any one piece should have some specific ranking. Yet if I had to choose, it seems to me that of all the pieces, the key one is the breastplate of righteousness. If there is no righteousness in your life, there is a good chance you won't be committed. If you are not committed to genuine righteousness in your life, you won't have the shield of faith,

79

the shoes of peace, the helmet of salvation, or the sword of the Spirit. One way of defining righteousness is having a right relationship to God. True commitment is born out of that relationship.

C. The Protection

1. The vital areas

In the kinds of battles the Romans were in, they needed to protect the area from the neck to the thighs. The helmet would protect the head. When the Romans fought in hand-to-hand combat, they used a short sword. It wasn't the kind that could cut off a head, so they endeavored to protect the area around the heart and the areas below that, which the Jewish people called "the bowels." That was the section where the functional organs of the body were located. So the breastplate covered two vital areas: the heart and the bowels.

a) The heart

To the Jew, the heart symbolically represented the mind.

(1) Proverbs 23:7—"For as [a man] thinketh in his heart, so is he."

(2) Mark 7:21—"Out of the heart of men, proceed evil thoughts."

(3) Jeremiah 17:9—"The heart is deceitful above all things, and desperately wicked."

b) The bowels

When the Hebrew referred to the bowels, he was referring to feelings and emotions. The Bible talks about shutting up the bowels of compassion and not loving someone properly (1 John 3:17). We ache in our stomach when we feel certain emotions. That's why the Hebrew thought the bowels were a good way to demonstrate emotions.

The heart refers to the thinking processes and the bowels refer to the emotions.

2. The vicious attack

Satan wants to attack a believer in two areas primarily: his thinking and his emotions. The believer must be protected in those areas. Satan feeds your mind and your emotions with false information. He wants to cloud your mind with false doctrine, lies, and religious untruth. He wants to elicit evil emotional responses from you and pervert your affections. But if you protect your mind and your heart from the attacks of Satan, you'll be impregnable. He will try to confuse your mind with false doctrine, or confuse your emotions by making you lust after wrong things.

The mind and the emotions together encompass everything that causes us to act: our knowledge, understanding, conscience, will, desires, drives, affections, feelings, and emotions. All those things are protected by the breastplate of righteousness.

a)   On the mind

Satan wants to snatch the Word of God from you and fill your mind with lies, perversion, immorality, false doctrine, untruths, and half-truths. He doesn't want you to interpret things correctly. He wants you to say that sin is not so bad. He tries to drown you in a sea of sin so that you become very tolerant of it. He tries to entertain you with sin so that you won't think it's as evil as it really is. He makes people laugh at sin on television or at the movies. He puts sin to beautiful music so that it confuses your mind. He also tries to destroy your conscience—to get you to do things you shouldn't do. He attempts to sear the conscience that once warned you so it will warn you no longer. He wants to debilitate your will.

b)   On the emotions

Satan wants to confuse your emotions by corrupting your desires and drawing your affections to the wrong things.

This attack of Satan comes to the mind and emotions. The apostle Paul says that those vital areas are protected by the breastplate of righteousness. Protect your thinking and feelings, and you will be impregnable against Satan.

D.   The Possibilities

What is the righteousness that Paul is referring to? There are only three possibilities to consider: one, our own self-righteousness; two, imputed righteousness, which is the righteousness that Christ has given to us; and three, practical righteousness, which involves living out the righteousness of Christ.

1. Self-righteousness

   There are people who think they're righteous just because they're good people. But what is Satan's ultimate
   goal? Drawing men into eternal hell with him to keep
   them from going to God. He does not want to populate
   God's kingdom—he does not want people bowing to
   Jesus Christ; he does not want citizens of heaven—he
   wants to populate his own dominion. Satan's ultimate
   goal is to destroy men. But there are some people who
   say, "My own righteousness will be sufficient to prevent
   that." Satan wants to ruin lives, yet there are people who
   think they can handle him.

   a) Of the scribes and Pharisees

      The scribes and the Pharisees thought they were
      good enough to reach heaven.

      (1) Matthew 5:20—Jesus said, "Except your righ-
          teousness shall exceed the righteousness of the
          scribes and Pharisees, ye shall in no case enter
          into the kingdom of heaven." They weren't good
          enough. Ephesians 2:8-9 says, "For by grace are
          ye saved through faith; and that not of your-
          selves, it is the gift of God—not of works." You
          can't make it on your own. Yet they thought they
          could.

      (2) Luke 18:10-14—The typical legalistic attitude of a
          Pharisee is exhibited by people today who think
          they can get to heaven by their own goodness.
          Every religious system in the world apart from
          Christianity is based on that assumption. The
          Lord tells this parable: "Two men went up into
          the temple to pray; the one a Pharisee, and the
          other a tax collector. The Pharisee stood and
          prayed thus with himself, God, I thank thee that
          I am not as other men are, extortioners, unjust,
          adulterers, or even as this tax collector. I fast
          twice in the week [the Jewish people were re-
          quired to fast only several times a year]; I give
          tithes of all that I possess. And the tax collector,
          standing afar off . . . smote upon his breast, say-
          ing, God be merciful to me a sinner. I tell you,
          this man went down to his house justified rather
          than the other; for everyone that exalteth himself
          shall be abased; and he that humbleth himself

shall be exalted." Another way of saying justified is "made righteous." Who was righteous: the man who thought he could be righteous on his own or the man who knew he couldn't? Jesus said that it was the man who knew he couldn't. You could title the story: "A good man who went to hell, and a bad man who went to heaven."

b) Of man

If you think you can be righteous on your own, you are self-righteous—and you do not have a breastplate. You will never defend yourself against Satan; he'll cast you into hell forever. Even though God has the ultimate right to send you to hell, Satan is the one who will lure you there. All your best efforts won't help.

(1) Isaiah 64:6—"All our righteousnesses are as filthy rags." That's the best we can offer. If you hope to get into heaven based on your goodness, you are the most deluded person of all.

(2) Romans 3:10-12, 19, 23—"As it is written, There is none righteous, no, not one: There is none that understandeth, there is none that seeketh after God. They are all gone out of the way, they are together become unprofitable; there is none that doeth good, no, not one" (vv. 10-12). The Greek word for "unprofitable" means "to go sour like milk." The human race has gone sour. As a result verse 19 says, "Every mouth [is] stopped, and all the world [is] guilty before God." Why? Verse 23 says, "For all have sinned, and come short of the glory of God." Self-righteousness is not the breastplate of righteousness. You will surely become a victim of the forces of hell if you try to cover yourself with your own righteousness.

c) Of the apostle Paul

In Philippians 3:4-6, Paul expresses his view of his self-righteousness. In verse 4 he says, "Though I might also have confidence in the flesh." In other words, "If self-righteousness were possible—if I could get into God's kingdom by being good enough—then I, of all people, would have a right to do so. I could have confidence in the flesh." Then he says, "If any other man thinketh that he hath reasons for which he might trust in the flesh, I more" (v. 4). In other words, "If you're going to examine human righteousness, I can do better than most." Why?

(1) His circumcision

Verse 5 says that Paul was "circumcised the eighth day of the stock of Israel." He was a real Israelite from circumcision, and it occurred on the right day.

(2) His tribe

Paul was "of the tribe of Benjamin" (v. 5). No tribe was more Jewish than the tribe of Benjamin. In the Old Testament, God dealt with them as a very special tribe. For example:

(a) According to Genesis 35:16-18, Benjamin was not only a son of Israel (Jacob) but also the son of Israel's most beloved wife Rachel.

(b) Of Israel's two favorite sons—Benjamin and Joseph—it was the tribe of Benjamin that formed the reconstituted nation of Israel with the tribe of Judah (1 Kings 12:21).

(c) The tribe of Benjamin restored the nation of Israel after the captivity (Ezra 4:1).

(d) The tribe of Benjamin was God's chief agent in delivering Israel from the wickedness of Haman during the time of Esther, the queen of Persia (Esther 2:5).

Benjamin was a very special tribe.

(3) His race

Verse 5 says that Paul was "an Hebrew of the Hebrews."

(4) His sect

Verse 5 also says Paul was "as touching the law, a Pharisee." He was not only a real Hebrew from the tribe of Benjamin but also a member of the strictest legalistic sect in the whole religious system—the Pharisees.

(5) His zeal

Verse 6 says, "Concerning zeal, persecuting the church."

(6) His righteousness

Verse 6 also says, "Touching the righteousness which is in the law, blameless."

If anyone could count on his self-righteousness, Paul had more going for him than anyone. If self-righteousness was the way into the kingdom, he could lay claim to it. But he couldn't—and no one can.

2. Imputed righteousness

a) In Paul's life

In Philippians 3:7-9 Paul says, "But what things were gain to me, those I counted loss for Christ. Yea doubtless, and I count all things but loss for the excellency of the knowledge of Christ Jesus, my Lord; for whom I have suffered the loss of all things, and do count them but refuse, that I may win Christ, and be found in him, not having mine own righteousness, which is of the law, but that which is through the faith of Christ, the righteousness which is of God by faith." In other words, "My own righteousness is useless; I must have the righteousness of God that comes by faith in Christ."

b) In the believer's life

When you become a Christian and reach out in faith to God through Christ, the righteousness of Christ is imputed to you at that moment: God clothes you in the righteousness of Christ. He puts a canopy of the absolute holiness of Jesus Christ over you. From that moment throughout eternity, whenever God looks at you, He sees the righteousness of Jesus Christ. Second Corinthians 5:21 says, "For he hath made him, who knew no sin, to be sin for us, that we might be made the righteousness of God in him." God sees you righteous in Christ. That is called *imputed righteousness* by the theologians. Your own righteousness is useless.

Eighteenth-century hymn writer Augustus Toplady said this in his hymn "A Debtor to Mercy Alone":

A debtor to mercy alone,
Of covenant mercy I sing,
Nor fear, with God's righteousness on,
My person and off'rings to bring.

The terrors of law and of God
With me can have nothing to do;
My Savior's obedience and blood
Hide all my transgressions from view.

God doesn't see our transgession as we stand clothed in the righteousness of Christ.

3. Practical righteousness

You can't be protected by the righteousness of your own life. Your breastplate is made of the righteousness that God granted to you at salvation. But there is one thing you must do.

a) In Paul's life

Paul recognized he had imputed righteousness, but he also realized there was something for him to do. In Philippians 3:10 he says, "That I may know him, and the power of his resurrection, and the fellowship of his sufferings, being made conformable unto his death." In verse 12 he says, "Not as though I had already attained, either were already perfect; but I follow after." Then in verse 13 he says, "Brethren, I count not myself to have apprehended." Finally, in verse 14 he says, "I press toward the mark." Paul recognized he had the imputed righteousness of Christ, but he knew he still had to press on, to learn, and move ahead. Imputed righteousness only makes practical righteousness possible; it doesn't necessarily make it a reality.

b) In the believer's life

When you were saved, you were given the righteousness of Jesus Christ. That righteousness will cover you for all eternity. But for you to live the kind of life that wins the battle over Satan, you must apply to your life the righteous principles that are available to you through Christ.

(1) Excusing sin

There are Christians who think that because they have the imputed righteousness of Christ, it doesn't matter what they do. My father told me about a man in the ministry who once swore a string of curse words when he was with him. In shock my father said, "Whatever possessed you to say that?" He said, "It doesn't matter; I'm covered by the righteousness of Christ. That's just my old nature. There's nothing I can do with it." On another occasion he told me of a man who had decided to visit a nude bar. Someone in his company said, "Why would you want to do that?" He replied, "I doesn't matter; I'm covered by the righteousness of Christ. That's just my old nature."

(2) Experiencing holiness

The righteousness of Christ and the old nature can't be separated. Although we are covered by the righteousness of Jesus Christ, that doesn't guarantee we will live every moment as we ought to; it only guarantees that we are able to. There's a difference between position and practice. Your position is secure forever, but your practice doesn't always match up with your position. Paul knew that because he had been given the righteousness of God didn't mean he had attained that righteousness in life. He knew he had to work out his salvation so he could accomplish what God wanted to do in his life (Phil. 2:12-13). The foundation is Christ, but you will be wearing the breastplate only when you are living a righteous and holy life.

Righteousness: A Glorious Dress

Count Zinzendorf, the eighteenth-century German leader of the Moravian Brethren, wrote the great hymn "Jesus, Thy Blood and Righteousness," which was translated by John Wesley:

Jesus, Thy blood and righteousness
My beauty are, my glorious dress;
'Midst flaming worlds, in these arrayed,
With joy shall I lift up my head.

Bold shall I stand in Thy great day,
For who aught to my charge shall lay?
Fully absolved through these I am,
From sin and fear, from guilt and shame.

O let the dead now hear Thy voice;
Now bid Thy banished ones rejoice;
Their beauty this, their glorious dress,
Jesus, Thy blood and righteousness.

He was right. The standard is Christ's righteousness, which covers us and was imputed to us. Romans 3:10 says that none are righteous, but verse 22 says that the righteousness of Christ is given to us. The perfection of Christ becomes ours so we can stand before God complete. We can never attain God's standard of righteousness on our own, so it comes as a gift from Jesus Christ.

Paul was not thinking of imputed righteousness for the breastplate of righteousness. As a Christian you have imputed righteousness, but you can constantly lose battles throughout your life. Paul was thinking of what the Puritans called "imparted righteousness"—you've got to put it to use. You live a righteous life through daily moment-by-moment choices. Practical righteousness is needed if you are to put all the armor on. In Philippians 3:14 Paul says that he wants to reach for the prize: Christlikeness. He wanted his practical righteousness to match his positional righteousness. Holy living is the breastplate.

E. The Problems

I believe that holiness is a forgotten commodity in the church. If you don't live a holy life, you lose.

1. Loss of joy and blessing

If you do not live a righteous life, God will withhold His blessings. First John 1:4 says, "These things write we unto you, that your joy may be full." They were written so that in obeying them, our joy will be full. No obedience; no joy. The reason Christians so often have sorrow in their lives is not a lack in psychological counseling for relational problems; it's simply a lack of personal holiness. Today, the church has ignored this problem and substituted programs, seminars, and counseling. If you have problems in your life, the first place to look for the cause is your holiness. If you have problems in your marriage, that's the first place to look. I'll guarantee you that if you're not living a holy life, you will have problems because God will withhold His blessing. David knew that to be true. When he was in sin, he said to the Lord, "Restore unto me the joy of thy salvation" (Ps. 51:12). He still had his slavation; he had just lost his joy.

Are You Wearing Paper Armor?

Today, I see Christians tying on paper armor. You may be familiar with the paper bib you put on little children when you eat out at a restaurant. I see that as the typical Christian breastplate. It's absolutely useless. It's made up of a system, method, or program. If someone is having problems in his family, he is told that he needs ten to twelve sessions with a counselor. That is a paper breastplate. But that's not what he needs. He needs about ten or twelve hours in the presence of God until he sorts out the unholy characteristics in his life and gets right with Him. We don't need more programs and methods; we need holiness in our lives. Our society is drowning in a sea of immorality, materialism, and humanism. It has engulfed and victimized us to the point that we easily bypass personal holiness. Even in the name of Jesus Christ and under the banner of ministries we substitute paper armor: programs, techniques, and methods. I call that Christian *stuff*. It has no lasting beneficial effect.

Check Your Holiness

Examine your life. Do you have problems in your family? Check your own holiness. Are you faithful in reading the Word of God? Is your prayer life what it ought to be? Are you loving your family the way you should? Are you speaking unashamedly for Jesus Christ in your society or culture? Are you giving sacrificially to the Lord what you ought and being a good steward of the rest of what you have? Are you living a righteous life as God has outlined in His Word? If you're not, why would you expect your life to go well? If it did, then God would defeat His own purposes.

The answers to our problems lie with our holiness. But most people want to find another answer. They would rather wear a paper breastplate than deal with the real issues. If there's disobedience and unconfessed sin in your life—such as wrong attitudes, resentment, and wrong thoughts, words, and deeds—you will have trouble. You will lose your joy.

2. Loss of fruitfulness

You will become unproductive. You will shrivel like a branch on the vine.

3. Loss of reward

John says, "Look to yourselves, that we lose not those things which we have wrought, but that we receive a full reward" (2 John 8). Some of you are going to diminish your capacity for serving God.

4. Loss of opportunity to glorify God

You bring reproach on God's glory when you're not holy. Why would you want to do that?

Are you so ungrateful to God that you would live a sinful and unrighteous life, forfeit the joy, say no to His gifts, and neglect what He wants to produce through your life? Would you restrict yourself by saying no to what He wants you to enjoy throughout all eternity in His heavenly kingdom? Would you say no to the God who seeks glory in the midst of men by living an unrighteous life that brings down His name? That is an affront to Him. God wants to fill us with blessings that include joy, fruitfulness, and ultimate rewards. Would you turn your back on His blessings and follow your own sinfulness instead? If you've got problems, they are directly related to your sin. But if things are right in your life and you're righteous before God, you may not have too many trials because there's not that much to refine. God has given simplicity in His Word. It is amazing to me that Christians ignore that and substitute a superficial answer for the clear bibilical solution.

F. The Plea

Get your armor on; this is war. I will go down with my last breath saying, "Lord, I want to win this last battle." I believe that God wants us to accomplish all we can, but that involves every one of us making the same commitment. In 1 Peter 2:11 Peter says, "Dearly beloved, I beseech you as sojourners and pilgrims, abstain from fleshly lusts which war against the soul." Peter is indicating that we are in a war, and we must be committed to righteousness. That doesn't mean you never sin; it means that there is a decreasing frequency of sin. When you sin, you confess it and repent of it. You deal with it before God.

1. Negative

Peter says, "Abstain from fleshly lusts which war against the soul." When you fall to those lusts, you lose your joy, fruitfulness, reward, and ultimately God's honor in the world. That is Peter's negative plea.

2. Positive

Peter's positive plea is in verse 12: "[Strive to have] your behavior honest among the Gentiles." Be committed.

G. The Perspective

1. A citizen of heaven

Hebrews 11:13 says that the heroes of faith "confessed that they were strangers and pilgrims on the earth." We too are strangers and pilgrims on the earth, but we don't realize that enough. We have become locked into loving the things of the world (1 John 2:15). But the people of faith "looked for a city . . . whose builder and maker is God" (Heb. 11:10). Paul said this to the Philippians: "Our citizenship is in heaven" (Phil. 3:20). Jesus tells us that we don't belong in the world. It hates us. We're not of the world; we have no part in it (John 15:18-19). Yet we become entrenched in the world and lose the right perspective. We don't see ourselves living in the heavenlies, fighting a spiritual warfare, and pursuing a righteous life, dependent on God's resources. It is stupid for a Christian to become engulfed in the world system.

2. A soldier of God

In 2 Timothy 2:3 Paul says, "Endure hardness, as a good soldier of Jesus Christ." We are to take it when it's tough. Then verse 4 says, "No man that warreth entangleth himself with the affairs of this life." Paul is saying this: You can't be in the army and be a civilian. You can't be both. If you have come to fight for the Commander and serve the Lord, then get out of the system. Instead, present your bodies as living sacrifices, holy and acceptable to God (Rom. 12:1). In Colossians 3:2 Paul says, "Set your affection on things above, not on things on the earth."

We have to put on the breastplate. In 1 Corinthians 15:34 Paul says, "Awake to righteousness, and sin not." Even the littlest sin can hurt. When a commander is about to engage in battle with another army, the first thing he does is send out an advance group. They are to establish a beachhead. From there, infiltration into enemy lines takes place. Satan wants to find one little weak crack in the dam of your armor. That's all he needs to burst the whole dam. The Bible says that it's "the little foxes, that

91

spoil the vines" (Song of Sol. 2:15). And remember this: You are going to win in the end. You will be victorious. There is no sense in forfeiting all the great things that God has for you now.

John Newton, the eighteenth-century hymn writer and clergyman wrote this:

> Though many foes beset you round,
> And feeble is your arm
> Your life is hid with Christ in God,
> Beyond the realm of harm.
>
> Weak as you are, you shall not faint,
> Or fainting, shall not die;
> Jesus, the strength of every saint,
> Will aid you from on high.
>
> Though unperceived by mortal sense,
> Fate sees Him always near,
> A guide, a glory, a defense:
> Then what have you to fear?
>
> As surely as He overcame,
> And triumphed once for you,
> So surely you that love His name
> Shall in Him triumph too!

Focusing on the Facts

1. Why is every Christian a potential loser in his daily battles with Satan (see p. 77)?
2. Based on Luke 14:31, what should every Christian be doing to prepare for his battle with Satan (see p. 77)?
3. What is one of the dangers that can occur as the church begins to grow (see p. 78)?
4. Describe the different kinds of breastplates the Romans would use in battle (see p. 79).
5. How can the breastplate of righteousness be viewed as the key piece of armor for the Christian (see p. 79)?
6. What areas was the Roman breastplate designed to protect? What did those areas symbolically represent for the Hebrew (see p. 80)?
7. What are the two areas of the believer that Satan wants to attack? Describe how he attacks those areas (see pp. 80-81).
8. What are the three possible types of righteousness Paul could be referring to in the breastplate of righteousness (see p. 81)?
9. What is Satan's goal for every individual (see p. 82)?

10. Explain how the scribes and Pharisees manifested an attitude of self-righteousness (see p. 82).
11. What is the best that man can offer God (Isa. 64:6; see p. 83)?
12. What will happen to the man who tries to cover himself with his own righteousness (see p. 83)?
13. Give the reasons Paul had used for once having confidence in his self-righteousness (Phil. 3:4-6; see pp. 83-85).
14. Why can the tribe of Benjamin be considered special (see p. 84)?
15. According to Philippians 3:7-9, what did Paul recognize about his own self-righteousness (see p. 85)?
16. Define imputed righteousness (2 Cor. 5:21; see p. 85).
17. What did Paul recognize that he had to do, despite having imputed righteousness (Phil. 3:10-14; see p. 86)?
18. What must every believer do to win the battle over Satan (see p. 86)?
19. To what kind of righteousness does the breastplate of righteousness refer (see p. 88)?
20. What does God withhold from the believer when he doesn't live a righteous life (see p. 88)?
21. What things in society have caused many Christians to bypass personal holiness (see p. 89)?
22. Describe the negative and positive pleas that Peter makes in 1 Peter 2:11-12 (see pp. 90-91).
23. What is your status on the earth (Heb. 11:13)? What is your status in heaven (Phil. 3:20; see p. 91)?

Pondering the Principles

1. Review the comments on commitment on pages 78 and 79. What is your level of commitment within your church? Are you at the core of involvement or are you on the peripheral edges? If you are on the periphery, why are you there? God wants you to be committed. He wants you to have the desire to be where the action is the toughest. There is no limit to what He can do through you when you are committed to the battle. As a Christian, you need to become serious about the battle you are in.
2. Lamentations 3:22 says, "It is because of the Lord's mercies that we are not consumed." When God imputed the righteousness of Christ to you, you were no longer under God's wrath. Take this time to thank Him for His mercies. Thank Him for choosing you from before the foundation of the world (Eph. 1:4). Thank Him especially for His gift of Jesus Christ, who took the punishment

that was meant for you. As you pray, be conscious of the great love that God has for you.

3. Check out the level of your holiness. Are you faithful to read the Word of God daily? Is prayer a way of life for you? Are you speaking out unashamedly for Jesus Christ? Are you giving sacrificially to the Lord? Are you being a good steward of what God has given to you? Are you living according to God's Word? Are you regularly confessing and repenting of sin in your life? You need to be improving in all those areas if you want to minimize the problems in your life. Isolate the things you aren't practicing the way you should. Plan some practical steps that you can take to be more obedient. Ask God for His direction in implementing those steps.

6
The Believer's Armor—Part 3

Outline

Introduction
A. The Plan of Satan
   1. In the life of a believer
   2. In the life of Christ
   3. In the church
      a) The past
      b) The present
B. The Principles for Victory
   1. Recognize that Christ has defeated Satan
   2. Recognize the power of Christ in your life
   3. Resist Satan
   4. Don't give Satan a place in your life
      a) Don't be ignorant of Satan's devices
      b) Flee temptation
   5. Let Christ control your thought life

Review
 I. The Belt of Truthfulness
 II. The Breastplate of Righteousness

Lesson
III. The Shoes of the Gospel of Peace
   A. The Function of Shoes
      1. In general
      2. In specific
         a) For the athlete
         b) For the Roman soldier
            (1) Protection
            (2) Stability
         c) For the Christian
   B. The Fundamentals for Standing
      1. The preparation

a) Identified
b) Interpreted
  (1) Improperly
  (2) Properly
2. The gospel of peace
  a) Its importance
    (1) Man's evil record
    (2) God's expedient remedy
  b) Its illustrations
    (1) Peter
    (2) Gideon
    (3) Peter and John
    (4) The apostle Paul

Introduction

Ephesians 6:13-17 is the setting for the theme of the believer's armor: "Wherefore, take unto you the whole armor of God, that ye may be able to withstand in the evil day, and having done all, to stand. Stand, therefore, having your loins girded about with truth, and having on the breastplate of righteousness, and your feet shod with the preparation of the gospel of peace; above all, taking the shield of faith, with which ye shall be able to quench all the fiery darts of the wicked. And take the helmet of salvation, and the sword of the Spirit, which is the word of God."

There was a time in the life of Martin Luther when his conflict with Satan became so very real that it took on a physical manifestation for him. In anger over Satan, Martin Luther picked up his inkwell and threw it at him. It broke, and splattered ink all over his wall. The stain remained for many years, reminding many people of how vivid the conflict had been in his life. It is no less real in our lives, though we may not have the spiritual intensity of Martin Luther. The believer and Satan are in mortal combat. Ephesians 6:12 says, "We wrestle." That verb describes a life-and-death, hand-to-hand combat.

A. The Plan of Satan

1. In the life of a believer

   God has such high and holy purposes for believers that He calls us to walk in a manner that sets us apart from the world's system. The living out of those purposes gain God His glory. But Satan does, and will continue to do, all he can to hinder us from realizing the purposes of God. Consequently, there's war in the life of a believer. I

96

believe the war begins at the moment of salvation. Before salvation can occur, the message of the gospel comes to a man. According to the words of our Lord, Satan attempts to snatch that message away so a person can't respond (Matt. 13:19). When a believer is just a little child in the faith, Satan sends a flood of false doctrine his way to toss him to and fro and carry him away from the truth (Eph. 4:14). He batters, besieges, and accuses us relentlessly throughout our lifetime.

2. In the life of Christ

When Jesus entered the world as a man, Satan tried to have Him murdered by Herod. He did everything he could during the life of Christ to have Him killed, including trying to push Him off a cliff and having Him crucified. But Jesus conquered all those efforts.

3. In the church

a) The past

The book of Acts indicates that as the church began to convey the message of Jesus Christ, the devil resisted them continually. The apostle Paul went on several missionary journeys to take the gospel to the world. He often ran into magicians, sorcerers, and demon-possessed people trying to thwart that effort. Some days after the day of Pentecost, Peter faced hostility. Persecution soon broke out against the church (Acts 4). On one occasion the Sanhedrin questioned Peter and the other disciples, and told them to keep silent about Christ (Acts 4:5-22). Throughout the New Testament, we see the gospel being withstood by Satan.

The first three centuries were fraught with persecutions of the church, including the martyrdom of those who love the Lord. The church then entered into the terror of the Dark Ages. The testimony of the gospel was almost blotted out, except for a few flickers of faithful groups who believed the truth throughout that time. Finally, during the time of the Reformation, the light dawned again. The gospel rang out loud and clear as the birth of the Protestant church took place. Then war occurred between Romanism and the Protestant church.

b) The present

Finally, we come to our own day. The gospel continues to be preached. But now modernism, liberalism, neo-orthodoxy, psychology, communism, humanism, materialism, and hedonism are encroaching on Protestantism.

From the beginning of the church until now, we can see a terrible battle between Satan and the gospel of Christ. But it isn't just a battle of movements or ideologies; it's a battle that occurs in the life of every individual. Satan assaults the work that God is attempting to accomplish in the life of His children. There is a war going on. That's why Paul closes Ephesians by describing the armor of the Christian. We know we have resources and that we are to walk worthy, but there is going to be resistance.

Satan's Opposition to Christ

Satan opposes everything God does. For example:

1. Jesus reveals the truth. John 1:17 says that grace and truth were realized in Him. But Satan conceals the truth. John 8:44 says, "He is a liar, and the father of [lies]."

2. John 5:24 says that Jesus gives life. Christ said that the Father had given life to Him, and that He would give life to whomever He wills. But in John 8:44 Satan is called a murderer. He takes life. Hebrews 2:14 says the devil has the power of death.

3. Jesus produces spiritual fruit in our lives. According to Galatians 5:22-23 He produces love, joy, peace, patience, gentleness, goodness, faith, meekness, and self-control. But according to Galatians 5:19-21 Satan produces fleshly fruit such as adultery, fornication, uncleanness, lasciviousness, idolatry, sorcery, hatred, strife, jealousy, wrath, factions, seditions, heresies, envyings, murders, drunkenness, and wild parties.

4. Jesus tests us so that we might become mature. James 1:3 says that the trying of our faith makes us perfect. But Satan tempts us to destroy us. Peter says that "the devil, like a roaring lion walketh about, seeking whom he may devour" (1 Pet. 5:8).

5. John 8:31-32 says that if you know the Son, He will make you free. But according to 2 Timothy 2:26, Satan wants to make you a slave.

6. In 1 John 2:1 Jesus defends the believer: "If any man sin, we have an advocate with the Father, Jesus Christ the righteous." But in Revelation 12:10 the devil accuses us.

Tremendous conflict is going on all the time between God and Satan in the life of a believer.

B. The Principles for Victory

How are we going to obtain victory? How do we get beyond our doubts, rise above our sins, supersede our indifferences, attain the level of spiritual life that God calls us to, and walk worthy of our heavenly calling? How do we defeat Satan? The New Testament gives us several key answers. I want to give you a mini-theology lesson on how a believer deals with Satan. There are people today who want to advocate exorcisms and other rituals and formulas for dealing with Satan, but you only need to know what the Scripture says.

1. Recognize that Christ has defeated Satan

First John 3:8 says that Jesus came to destroy the works of the devil. Hebrews 2:14-15 says the plan was "that through death he might destroy him that had the power of death, that is, the devil, and deliver them who, through fear of death, were all their lifetime subject to bondage." The Lord has already dealt a defeating blow.

2. Recognize the power of Christ in your life

The power that defeated Satan dwells in you. First John 4:4 says, "Greater is he that is in you, than he that is in the world." When a believer is saved, he receives the Spirit of God, in whom is the power that defeated Satan.

3. Resist Satan

First Peter 5:8-9 says, "Be sober [know your priorities, be committed], be vigilant, because your adversary, the devil, like a roaring lion walketh about, seeking whom he may devour; whom resist steadfast in the faith." Principle one is to recognize that Christ has already dealt a death blow to Satan. Principle two is to recognize that the power that defeated Satan is in you by the Spirit of God. Principle three is to resist Satan because you have the power to do so. But you ask, "How do you resist him?"

4. Don't give Satan a place in your life

Ephesians 4:27 tells us we can resist Satan by expressing

God's power in our lives: "Neither give place to the devil." That's very simple; don't give him a place in your life. The implication of that verse is if he has a place in your life, then you gave it to him. Your will is the key. People will say that someone is so troubled by demons he can't use his will. But that can't be possible because we're called to give no place to the devil—to allow no room for his entry. You ask, "How do I keep from doing that?"

a) Don't be ignorant of Satan's devices

Second Corinthians 2:11 says "[Beware] lest Satan should get an advantage of us; for we are not ignorant of his devices." If you don't want to give him a place, then be aware of where he's coming from. You say, "What are his devices?" First John 2:16 says, "For all that is in the world, the lust of the flesh, and the lust of the eyes, and the pride of life, is not of the Father, but is of the world." The lust of the eyes, the lust of the flesh, and the pride of life are Satan's devices. If you're not ignorant of them, you effectively bar him from your life in those areas. When you give no place to Satan, you will resist his entry into your life.

b) Flee temptation

Second Timothy 2:22 says, "Flee also youthful lusts, but follow righteousness."

That's a simple formula. You ask, "How do you orient yourself to do it?"

5. Let Christ control your thought life

Second Corinthians 10:3 says, "For though we walk in the flesh, we do not war after the flesh." Paul is saying that we are human, but our battle is not human. Verse 4 says, "For the weapons of our warfare are not carnal, but mighty through God." We are in a spiritual war that demands spiritual weapons. How are we going to use those weapons? How do we know we can be aware of his devices, flee his temptations, resist his onslaughts, and give no place to him in our lives? How are we going to appropriate the necessary power? Verse 5 says by "bringing into captivity every thought to the obedience of Christ." For us to know that Christ has dealt a death blow to Satan, that His power resides in us, and to know how to resist Satan and give no place to his entry, we must bring every thought captive to Christ. We must have our minds controlled by the Word of God through the power of the Spirit of God. There are no short cuts to effective, victorious Christian living. If you're going to live a victorious Christian life, you must give your mind over to the Word of God so that your thinking and feelings are controlled by truth.

Those principles are the New Testament formula for victory. They are all beautifully summarized in one passage: Ephesians 6:13-17. This passage is a masterpiece that describes how a believer wins the war against the forces of hell. Remember, there is a real war, but real victory is available on a day-to-day basis.

Review

As Paul examines the Christian's war with Satan, he pictures a Roman soldier ready for battle. That soldier's preparation provides Paul with the imagery he uses to illustrate the Christian's battle with Satan.

I. THE BELT OF TRUTHFULNESS (v. 14a; see p. 65)

When the Roman soldier pulled his loose-fitting robe together with his belt, he was making a commitment to fight. It was a sign of preparedness, readiness, anticipation, and sincerity. Paul said, "Stand, therefore, having your loins girded about with truth" (v. 14). A believer must have a commitment to the truth. He must fight the fight and live the life, having the necessary dedication and consecration to win the battle.

II. THE BREASTPLATE OF RIGHTEOUSNESS (v. 14b; see p. 79)

Verse 14 says, "Having on the breastplate of righteousness." A Roman soldier put on a breastplate to cover his vital areas. If he was struck there, it could have been fatal. He was protecting his heart and his visceral area. To the Hebrews, the heart symbolized the mind and the visceral area or bowels symbolized the feelings. The believer needs to protect his mind and feelings because Satan brings temptations in those areas. He wants to induce us to sin. That's why we must protect those areas with the breastplate of righteousness. As we live a holy life—a consecrated, righteous life—we protect our vital areas from the terrible attacks of Satan.

We need to seek daily to be holy and righteous. We need to be confessing and repenting of sin in our lives. That is an injunction in the New Testament.

1. 1 Peter 1:16—"Be ye holy; for I am holy."

2. 2 Corinthians 7:1—"Let us cleanse ourselves from all filthiness of the flesh and spirit, perfecting holiness in the fear of God."

3. Colossians 3:5—Paul says we are to kill the evil desires of the body.

4. 1 Thessalonians 5:22—"Abstain from all appearance of evil."

5. Romans 13:11-14—"Knowing the time, that now it is high time to awake out of sleep; for now is our salvation nearer than when we believed [the coming of Christ is closer]. The night is far spent, the day [the great Day of the Lord] is at hand; let us, therefore, cast off the works of darkness, and let us put on the armor of light" (vv. 11-12). That is what Paul is saying in Ephesians 6. The light signifies holiness and purity, and darkness signifies evil. Casting off the works of darkness and putting on the armor of light is the same as putting on the breastplate of righteousness. Then Paul says, "Let us walk honestly, as in the day" (v. 13). That's the belt of commitment and truth: We are to live without hypocrisy, committed to win, and willing to be exposed because we are upright and honest as we battle for the Lord. Then Paul says, "Not in reveling and drunkenness, not in immorality and wantonness [living without shame], not in strife and envying. But put ye on the Lord Jesus Christ, and make not provision for the flesh, to fulfill its lusts" (vv. 13-14). When Paul describes the breastplate of righteousness, he is saying the same thing: Get rid of evil and enjoy a holy and righteous relationship with the Lord. That doesn't mean we're going to be perfect. We're to strive to be perfect, but we will fail. When we do sin, we are to confess it and repent of it.

Lesson

III. THE SHOES OF THE GOSPEL OF PEACE (v. 15)

"And your feet shod with the preparation of the gospel of peace."

A. The Function of Shoes

1. In general

Shoes have become a major part of our culture. Originally they were used to protect feet, but now they've become a fashion item. Frankly, we don't need that much protection for our feet. Our streets are paved. Our cars, churches, and offices are carpeted. The places that aren't carpeted have fairly clean floors. For the most part, we aren't walking over rough stones, wading through mud, tramping through dust, or strolling across thorny bushes. We need to understand how terrible the terrain was during the time of Christ. It was hard to walk over cobbles, rocks, pebbles, and thorns in those parts of the world. We might appreciate the need more by understanding that we need shoes for hiking, tramping across the desert, or walking on a hot pavement.

2. In specific

a) For the athlete

Today we have shoes for every conceivable sport. Each shoe serves a specific function. If you're participating in a sport that's played on concrete, you need to have a certain kind of shoe. If you're playing on dirt, you need another kind of shoe. There are different shoes for tennis depending upon the surface. Some matches are played on grass courts, some on clay courts, and some on concrete courts. There are shoes designed for wood floors. There are different track shoes for a cinder track or a rubberized track.

When I was playing football in college, one of our games took place at the Rose Bowl. It had been raining for a couple of weeks before the game, and the field was in bad shape. Once the field gets a lot of play toward the end of the season, the grass is basically gone. When it rains, there is a real problem. The grounds crew will paint the field green so it looks grassy. When we got to the field, it looked pretty good. We didn't know what kind of shape it was in.

103

I had two pairs of football shoes, one with long spikes for bad turf and one with short spikes for good turf. I figured the field was in good enough condition, and since the long spikes were heavy, I wore the short spikes. That was the wrong choice. My shoes were inadequate. I didn't discover that until the kickoff. I was standing on the four-yard line waiting to receive the opening kickoff and return it. I gathered the ball in, took about two steps, and landed on my southern hemisphere in front of the whole stadium! I sat there with the ball gently cradled in my lap while twenty-one people stared down at me, none of whom had even touched me. I felt all alone. We had to start play from scrimmage on our own eight-yard line. I realized then that I should have worn my other shoes. I even tried to get someone who didn't play as frequently to swap shoes with me, but I couldn't get any takers. As a result, I slipped all over the field.

b) For the Roman soldier

Shoes do provide a certain function, and that is especially true in war. If it is important to have the right shoe in athletics, you can imagine how important it would be if you were fighting for your life. A Roman soldier wouldn't go into a battle wearing an ordinary leather shoe with a slick bottom. If he did, he would slip and slide. If he had to climb a rock to fight an enemy, he would slip on the rock. That's why the soldier had to have special shoes. They could possibly save his life. The soldier's footwear served several functions.

(1) Protection

The Roman soldier had to have the kind of shoe that would last for long marches. He would often cover tremendous amounts of terrain. Many battles have been lost because soldiers didn't have adequate shoes. During the American Revolutionary War, the soldiers under General Washington wrapped their feet because their shoes had worn out. The soldiers couldn't protect their feet from being frozen or injured.

(2) Stability

During the time of the Roman wars, a method similar to the mine fields of modern warfare was used to trap approaching armies. A certain army would place razor-sharp sticks in the ground facing the approaching army in hopes of piercing the feet of the soldiers. To protect themselves, Roman soldiers would wear a boot with a heavy sole that couldn't be pierced. If a soldier's feet were pierced, he couldn't walk. He could be the best soldier in the army, but if the bottom of his feet were injured, he couldn't fight. He could hurt his arms, hands, elbows, shoulders and still keep moving, but if he hurt his feet, he was debilitated. Even the greatest soldier was useless if he couldn't stand up.

The Roman soldier wore a thick-soled, hobnailed, semi-boot. It had straps that tied around the foot so that it was tight. On the bottom of the soles were hobnails—little pieces of metal that protruded like a football, track, or baseball shoe—to give them a grip on the soil. This shoe gave him firmness of footing so he could stand in the battle. Paul pictures a Roman soldier standing firm, able to hold his ground and make quick moves without slipping, sliding, or falling.

c) For the Christian

Christians need to have shoes, too. You can have your waist cinched up with commitment and be wearing the breastplate of a godly and righteous life, but unless you can stand on your feet, you're going to fall. That's why you must have a solid base.

B. The Fundamentals for Standing

1. The preparation

a) Identified

Your feet are to be shod with "the preparation of the gospel of peace." The word *preparation* need not confuse you. It is an awkward translation. It simply means, "made ready or equipped." Paul is saying that your feet should be made ready by being shod. They should be equipped and prepared. In Titus 3:1 the same Greek word for "preparation" is translated "ready." Our feet should be equipped—properly shod for the battle.

b) Interpreted

(1) Improperly

Many commentators who have written on this subject assume that *preparation* refers to preaching the gospel of peace. They reach that interpretation based on Romans 10:15, which quotes Isaiah 52:7: "And how shall they preach, except that they be sent? As it is written, How beautiful are the feet of them that preach the gospel of peace, and bring glad tidings of good things!" There is no question that the gospel of peace is something to be preached. That's what Paul is saying in Romans 10:15, but that is not what he is saying in Ephesians 6:15. It has nothing to do with preaching or going anywhere.

(2) Properly

The first word in Ephesians 6:14 is *stand*. Paul is not talking about going; he's talking about standing. Paul is not referring to evangelizing the lost or preaching the gospel; he is referring to fighting the devil. The idea is best expressed in the words of 1 Corinthians 16:13, "Stand fast in the faith." Ephesians 6:11 says, "That ye may be able to stand." Verse 13 says, "That ye may be able to withstand in the evil day, and having done all, to stand." Those verses are about standing, not about going. Certainly the gospel of peace is to be preached, and the feet of those who go and preach are beautiful, but that's not the proper interpretation of Ephesians 6:15. This verse refers to the believer in conflict with Satan. Paul is saying that since our feet are shod with the good news of peace, we can stand our ground. We don't need to slip, slide, or fall when we're under attack.

2. The gospel of peace

What does the phrase "the gospel of peace" mean? The word *gospel* means "good news," so the phrase means "the good news of peace." What exactly is the good news of peace?

106

a) Its importance

(1) Man's evil record

Romans 5:6 gives the basic picture of man: "For when we were yet without strength." Man is weak. Verse 7 says, "For scarcely for a righteous man will one die." That means no one would die for an unrighteous man. The implication is that we are weak and unrighteous. Verse 8 says, "While we were yet sinners, Christ died for us." That defines us as sinners. Verse 9 says, "Much more than, being now justified by his [Christ's] blood, we shall be saved from wrath through him." That indicates we were unjust, unsaved, and the objects of God's wrath. That is a good definition of man: He is weak, unrighteous, sinful, unjust, unsaved, and an object of wrath. Verse 10 sums up man's status: "For if, when we were enemies." A man who is weak, unrighteous, sinful, unjust, and unsaved is an enemy of God and the object of God's judgment.

God and man are on two different sides. Don't let anyone tell you that God is the Father of everyone, that He tolerates everyone, and that everyone is in His family. Nahum 1:3 says, "The Lord . . . will not at all acquit the wicked." God is a God of vengeance and justice. If a man and a woman are enemies of God, they will feel His judgment. But what did God do to change that situation?

(2) God's expedient remedy

Romans 5:6-8 says that when we were weak, "in due time Christ died for the ungodly. For scarcely for a righteous man will one die; yet perhaps for a good man some would even dare to die. But God commendeth his love toward us in that, while we were yet sinners, Christ died for us." God is saying, "You're enemies, but I'm going to try to remedy that in the death of Christ." Then verses 9-10 say, "Being now justified by his blood, we shall be saved from wrath through him. For if, when we were enemies, we were reconciled to God by the death of his Son."

The gospel of peace is this: Man was at war with God, but Christ made peace. Romans 5:1 says, "Therefore, being justified by faith, we have peace with God through our Lord Jesus Christ." Man and God were at war. Jesus said, "He that is not with me is against me" (Matt. 12:30). In Revelation 2:16 the Lord says, "I will come unto thee quickly, and will fight against them with the sword of my mouth." Man is an enemy of God, yet Christ makes peace a reality. That's the good news.

We are at peace with God—we aren't on opposite sides anymore. God is on our side. We are reconciled. Second Corinthians 5:19 says that God has reconciled us to Him. Colossians 1:20-21 says, "And, having made peace through the blood of his cross, by him to reconcile all things unto Himself. . . . And you, that were once alienated and enemies in your mind by wicked works, yet now hath he reconciled." We are one with God; He is on our side. That means a Christian who stands firm can say, "Satan, you can come against me, but I have shoes that anchor me to the ground. God is on my side." That's what helps us stand. If I had to fight the host of hell in my own strength, I would lose.

b) Its illustrations

(1) Peter

In John 18 Peter stood with the disciples while the soldiers came to capture Christ. There were probably five hundred of them who marched from Fort Antonius. They carried torches to light the night so they could find Jesus. They assumed He would be hiding in a cave somewhere in the garden. They also carried clubs and staves to beat Him into submission and to fight off His disciples. But Jesus stepped out to meet them and said, "Whom seek ye? They answered him, Jesus, of Nazareth. Jesus saith unto them, I am he" (vv. 4-5). When He said that, they fell over like a bunch of dominoes (v. 6). After they got back up and dusted themselves off, He again said, "Whom seek ye? And they said Jesus of

Nazareth" (v. 7). When they had first fallen to the ground, no doubt Peter thought, "What power! Just His name caused what seemed like the whole Roman army to collapse. Since He is that powerful, there's no sense in being taken." The Bible says that he grabbed his sword and chopped off the ear of the servant of the high priest (v. 10). He was not trying to chop off Malchus's ear; I'm convinced he was aiming for his head. Malchus probably just ducked. But that's not the whole story. Peter was intending to fight the whole Roman army. You say, "Where did he get that kind of confidence?" He had just seen a bunch of soldiers fall flat in the dirt at the very name of Jesus. Peter was thinking, "If I get in any trouble, I'll just say, 'Get them, Jesus!' " He had a sense of invincibility. He sensed that nothing could ever defeat him because he had seen the power of Christ displayed. That's why he took the sword and tried to defend the Lord. He knew Christ was on his side.

(2) Gideon

In Judges 6 the host of Midian came to attack the children of Israel. God moved on the hearts of Israel to fight against the Midianites, so the people assembled an army of thirty-two thousand soldiers. But the Lord told Gideon that He didn't need thirty-two thousand soldiers (Judg. 7:2). He told him to eliminate everyone who was fearful. Eventually three hundred men remained. The Lord told Gideon that those men would defeat the host of Midian (v. 7). So He told Gideon to give each man a pitcher covering a candle, and a trumpet. Then they were to circle the host of Midian encamped in the valley below them. When God gave Gideon the word, the men were to blow their trumpets, break their pitchers, and hold up their candles (vv. 16-21). Do you know what happened? When they followed the Lord's instructions, the host of Midian killed each other (v. 22). Gideon knew who was on his side.

(3) Peter and John

Peter and John told the council of the Sanhedrin that they couldn't obey the command to stop preaching because they were going to serve God (Acts 5:27-29). They had no fear because they knew who was on their side.

(4) The apostle Paul

Paul boldly preached Jesus Christ because he knew the resources that were his in Christ (Rom. 1:16). He was at peace with God. He knew God was on his side.

In Christ's power we stand. I can say to Satan, "Whatever you may cast against me, I have absolutely no fear because God's on my side." If I knew what I know about Satan, and didn't have God on my side, I would be scared all the time. You can stand in absolute confidence. Jesus Christ is not ashamed to call us brothers (Heb. 2:11). It is great to know that He's on our side. When Satan attacks, our feet are rooted firmly on the solid ground of the gospel of peace. The good news is that I'm not an enemy of God anymore. He is on my side because of Jesus Christ. No matter what Satan brings against me, I can "be strong in the Lord, and in the power of his might" (Eph. 6:10). That's the confidence you can have when your feet are shod with the preparation of the gospel of peace.

Victory is available in your life. Answer these three questions: Do you really want to win—are you wearing the belt of commitment? Do you seek to live a holy life—are you wearing the breastplate of righteousness? Are you bold in the battle because your feet are firmly rooted in confidence in God? If you're doubting the Lord and His strength, you're going to lose. But if you can answer those three questions affirmatively, then you're a winner and God will do exciting and revolutionary things in your life for His own glory.

Focusing on the Facts

1. Describe the ways Satan tries to hinder God's plan in the life of a believer (see p. 96).
2. Describe the obstacles that the church has had to face since it began to carry the gospel of Christ to the world (see p. 97).
3. What specific works of Christ does Satan oppose? Support your answers with Scripture (see pp. 98-99).
4. Give five principles for victory over Satan (see pp. 99-101).

5. Describe ways you can keep from giving Satan access to your life (see pp. 99-100).
6. What are the devices of Satan (1 John 2:16; see p. 100)?
7. What must a Christian do to be aware of Satan's devices, flee his temptations, resist his onslaughts, and give no place to him (see p. 100)?
8. What are some of the New Testament injunctions for daily living a holy life (see p. 102)?
9. What two functions were served by the Roman soldier's shoe? Explain each function (see pp. 104-5).
10. What does the word "preparation" mean as it is used in Ephesians 6:15 (see p. 106)?
11. How has Ephesians 6:15 been improperly interpreted? What is the proper interpretation (see p. 106)?
12. What does "the gospel of peace" mean (see p. 106)?
13. Give a definition of man based on Romans 5:6-10 (see p. 107).
14. According to Romans 5:6-10, how did God remedy man's situation (see pp. 107-8)?
15. What gave Peter the confidence that he could attack the Roman army without fear (John 18:4-10; see p. 109)?

Pondering the Principles

1. Review the five principles for gaining victory over Satan (see pp. 99-100). Answer these questions: Do you realize that Jesus destroyed the works of the devil on the cross and that His power resides in you? How do you manifest His power in your life? Do you resist Satan by not allowing him access to your life? Describe some of the ways that he is able to gain access. If you were not ignorant of his devices, and you fled temptation, would he still be able to gain access to your life? Do you allow Christ to control your thoughts? When you can effectively follow the principles for victory against Satan, you will experience victory on a daily basis. But you must be committed to follow those principles regularly for victory to become a reality.
2. Are you living a holy life on a daily basis? Examine your walk as a Christian. Which areas of your life are characterized by holiness? Which areas are not characterized by holiness? You should be striving to be perfect in all areas of your life, although there will be times when you fail. But your failure is not as important as your attitude when you do so. Do you get upset at yourself and promise to do better next time? Do you blame your failure on your old nature? Or do you confess your sin to God and strongly desire to repent of it? If you are doing the latter, then you have

the right attitude. If you are not, examine the reasons behind your present attitude. Then bring your sins before God. Confess them to Him and turn from them.

3. Read Romans 5:6-10. What were you like before God saved you? Would you ever save someone like that—someone who hated you and did evil against you continually? Yet that is how you once appeared to God. Based on that, find a quiet place and take some time to meditate on the magnitude of God's love for you. Offer up praise and thanksgiving to Him for providing a remedy to reconcile you with Himself. Thank Him for giving you a confident salvation.

7
The Believer's Armor—
Part 4

Outline

Introduction
A. The Positional Victory
1.   Romans 8:31-39
2.   1 Corinthians 15:57
3.   2 Corinthians 2:14
4.   1 John 5:5
B. The Practical Victory

Review
I. The Belt of Truthfulness
II. The Breastplate of Righteousness
III. The Shoes of the Gospel of Peace

Lesson
IV. The Shield of Faith
A. Describing the Roman Shield
1.   A small, round shield
2.   A large, wooden plank
a)   Its design
b)   Its defense
B. Describing the Shield of Faith
1.   Its enemy
a)   His character
b)   His weapons
2.   Its effectiveness
a)   The act of believing
b)   The work of temptation
(1) On Adam and Eve
(2) On Christ
(a)   Temptation #1
(b)   Temptation #2

(c) Temptation #3
(3) On believers today
c) The faith of obedience
(1) God's promises
(a) The resistance to obedience: unbelief
(b) The result of obedience: blessing
(2) God's shield
3. Its empowerment

Introduction

Ephesians 6:10-17 delineates the warfare of the Christian. Our manner of life in this world will be conflict against the enemy. But there's no reason for us to fear him because the victory is ours.

A. The Positional Victory

1. Romans 8:31-39—"What shall we then say to these things? If God be for us, who can be against us? He that spared not his own Son, but delivered him up for us all, how shall he not with him also freely give us all things?" (vv. 31-32). In other words, "Who can defeat us? Since God gave us Christ, wouldn't He give us any resource we needed to win the battle?" Verse 33 says, "Who shall lay any thing to the charge of God's elect? Shall God that justifieth?" Since God is the highest court and says we are just, who can accuse us? Verse 34 says, "Who is he that condemneth? Shall Christ that died, yea rather, that is risen again?" Since Christ rose again for our justification, is He then going to condemn us? Since God is the highest court and Christ the greatest judge and they have declared us just and righteous, who could possibly bring any accusation against us? The obvious answer is no one. Verses 35-39 say, "What shall separate us from the love of Christ? Shall tribulation, or distress, or persecution, or famine, or nakedness, or peril, or sword? As it is written, For thy sake we are killed all the day long; we are accounted as sheep for the slaughter. Nay, in all these things we are more than conquerors through him that loved us. For I am persuaded that neither death, nor life, nor angels, nor principalities, nor powers, nor things present, nor things to come, nor height, nor depth, nor any other creation, shall be able to separate us from the love of God, which is in Christ Jesus, our Lord." We

are superconquerors. We have more than victory; we have supervictory.

2. 1 Corinthians 15:57—"But thanks be to God, who giveth us the victory through our Lord Jesus Christ."

3. 2 Corinthians 2:14—"Now thanks be unto God, who always causeth us to triumph in Christ."

4. 1 John 5:5—"Who is he that overcometh the world, but he that believeth that Jesus is the Son of God?"

We are overcomers—trimphant, victorious, invincible, superconquerors in Christ. But that only refers to our positional victory in Christ.

B. The Practical Victory

To win the battle every day, we have to appropriate the armor that God has made available. When we appropriate it, we can be superconquerors on a day-to-day basis. We can go beyond winning the battle—we can take the spoil. We can go beyond claiming victory—we can inherit all the possessions of the vanquished foe.

Jehoshaphat the Superconqueror

In 2 Chronicles 20:22-23 Israel is going to battle: "And when they began to sing and to praise, the Lord set an ambush against the children of Ammon, Moab, and Mount Seir, who were come against Judah; and they were smitten. For the children of Ammon and Moab stood up against the inhabitants of Mount Seir, utterly to slay and destroy them; and when they had made an end of the inhabitants of Seir, everyone helped to destroy another." The Lord let all the enemies kill each other while Israel praised God; the Israelites never even fired a shot! The narrative continues: "And when Judah came toward the watchtower in the wilderness, they looked unto the multitude, and, behold, they were dead bodies fallen to the earth, and none escaped. And when Jehoshaphat and his people came to take away the spoil from them, they found among them in abundance both riches with the dead bodies, and precious jewels, which they stripped off for themselves, more than they could carry away; and they were three days in gathering the spoil, it was so much. And on the fourth day they assembled themselves in the valley of Beracah; for there they blessed the Lord. Therefore, the name of the same place was called, The Valley of Beracah, unto this day. Then they returned, every man of Judah and Jerusalem, and Jehoshaphat in the forefront of them, to go again to

Jerusalem with joy; for the Lord had made them rejoice over their enemies. And they came to Jerusalem with psalteries and harps and trumpets unto the house of the Lord. And the fear of God was on all the kingdoms of those countries, when they had heard that the Lord fought against the enemies of Israel" (vv. 24-29).

We have just seen a picture of superconquerors. First, they didn't even have to fight the battle. Second, when the battle was over, everyone in the enemy force was dead. Third, all the spoil was theirs. Then they returned to Jerusalem singing and praising God. Ultimately, verse 30 says, "God gave [them] rest round about." Their foe was absolutely obliterated, the spoil took three days to collect, and they returned with joy never having engaged in a fight. The whole victory was given by the Lord. That's what it is like to be a superconqueror. It is the same in the Christian life: God does all the fighting. He gives us the victory, lets us collect all the spoils, and enter into His presence with joy. God expects you to live with that kind of victorious approach to life.

To experience the positional reality in practical living, you must apply the armor of the Christian on a day-to-day basis. But how does a Christian daily appropriate all the armor? How do we experience the joy, exhilaration, and blessedness that Israel did when their battle was fought by the Lord? How can we be fully enriched by the spoils? The key is in Ephesians 6. As long as we wear the six pieces of the believer's armor, we will know the victory and spoil that belongs to superconquerors.

Review

I. THE BELT OF TRUTHFULNESS (v. 14a; see p. 65)

If we are going to fight Satan, we have to realize that he is a formidable foe. That means we have to be prepared. Girding up the loins was a symbol for preparation in Hebrew culture. In the same way a soldier must gird up his loins to do battle.

II. THE BREASTPLATE OF RIGHTEOUSNESS (v. 14b; see p. 79)

When we confess and repent of sin, we are maintaining personal holiness. That is what it means to put on the breastplate of righteousness. The breastplate covers the heart and the visceral area, the seat of the thoughts and emotions according to Hebrew thinking. Our thoughts and feelings are guarded by holiness and righteousness.

III. THE SHOES OF THE GOSPEL OF PEACE (v. 15; see p. 103)

Roman soldiers wore a type of sandal or half-boot that had hobnails sticking out of the sole. That helped them to stand firmly. The shoes that cause the Christian to stand firmly against Satan are made of the gospel of peace. That is the good news of our peace with God. We know that God is on our side. It was that confidence that enabled Peter to attack the Roman army in the Garden of Gethsemane (John 18:10). He knew Jesus could defeat the entire army if he got into trouble. As Christians we can stand our ground confident that God is on our side.

How do we defeat Satan's army—his host of demons? How do we stop the antagonistic attack from the kingdom of darkness? By commitment, holiness, and confidence that God's power and resources are sufficient.

Lesson

IV. THE SHIELD OF FAITH (v. 16)

Ephesians 6:16 says, "Above all, taking the shield of faith, with which ye shall be able to quench all the fiery darts of the wicked." Whatever the shield of faith is, it is sufficient because it quenches all the fiery darts of the wicked one. It is sufficient whatever the need.

A. Describing the Roman Shield

There were several kinds of shields used by different armies in Roman times, depending on the nature of the battle. Two stand out:

1. A small, round shield

This shield was like a giant frisbee, curled at the edges. It was usually strapped to the left forearm of the soldier. It was very light so it could be carried about by a foot soldier in battle. He would use it to parry the blows during hand-to-hand combat. He carried his sword in his right hand. This sword, according to verse 17, was a *machaira*, a Greek word meaning dagger. It was short—about eight to ten inches in length. In hand-to-hand combat, the soldier would strike with that sword while he parried the blows of his opponent with his shield. But that is not the kind of shield Paul was referring to in verse 16.

2. A large, wooden plank

117

a) Its design

The Greek word that Paul used to describe a completely different shield is *thureon*. This shield measured four-and-a-half feet by two-and-a-half feet. It was made out of a big thick plank of wood. It was covered on the outside with metal and sometimes even leather. This outer covering was very thick. The metal would deflect arrows, while the leather was treated with oil to extinguish the fiery pitch on the arrows.

In those days, people were much smaller than they are today. When I visited England and Scotland, I saw some suits of armor. Upon examining the armor the people wore, I wondered who could have fit into such small suits of armor. Obviously they were small people. And as far as we know, the same was true in the time of the Lord. In that case, a four-and-a-half by two-and-a- half foot shield would provide total protection. They only had to stick it in the ground and get behind it. So this shield was designed for full protection.

b) Its defense

When the Roman army fought, they would use a specific strategy for a major battle. A long line of soldiers that carried the shields would stand in front of the troops. Behind the shield bearers would be all the soldiers with swords and arrows. As the army moved toward the enemy, the soldiers in front would plant their shields side-by-side, creating a huge wall of protection. From behind that wall the archers would fire their arrows at the enemy. In this manner, the army inched its way towards the enemy until they could engage them in hand-to-hand combat. So the troops in the front would provide the wall that shielded the front line of the army from the enemy's barrage of arrows. It was true that the troops behind the front line also protected themselves with those shields. But you can imagine that if you didn't have a shield like that, and a barrage of arrows came from the enemy, you would be in danger of losing your life. However, your shield would protect you.

Double Protection for the Battle

Ephesians 6:16 begins with the words, "Above all." That does not mean the shield of faith is the most important piece of armor. Paul does not even deal with the issue of importance. All the pieces of armor are essential. But Paul is saying that in addition to your belt, your breastplate, and your shoes, to take "the shield of faith. . . . And take the helmet of salvation, and the sword of the Spirit" (vv. 16-17).

The phrase "above all" introduces the three remaining pieces of armor. There is a distinction in the verbs that introduce the pieces to show that there is a difference. In verse 14, Paul uses the verb "having"—having your loins girded, having your feet shod, and having on the breastplate. Paul is communicating something that is permanent. We are to wear those three pieces permanently as long-range preparation. If there was a lull in the battle, a soldier might rest, but he wouldn't take off his breastplate, belt, and shoes. But when the battle got hot, he would take his shield, helmet, and sword. If you have a commitment to the cause of Christ because your belt is on, absolute holiness in your life because your breastplate is on, and confidence in God's power because you've shod your feet with the gospel of peace, that would seem to be sufficient—and it is. But the remaining pieces provide a double protection that is useful when the battle gets furious.

The believer needs to keep the first three pieces of armor on all the time. As I was growing up, I remember going to conferences that were always calling for a rededication to Christ. I went to a school that held rededications all the time. There would be meetings month after month with someone speaking to the Christian students and calling for a recommitment. The same people would recommit their lives every time! They were simply going back to the three basics: commitment, righteousness, and confidence in God's power. Those are things they should have kept on all the time.

When a baseball player sits on the bench, he doesn't take his uniform off. He may have pads on for protection when sliding, and wear spikes on his feet. But when it is his turn to bat, he puts on a helmet and takes his bat. He had been prepared to bat, but now he takes the weapons of his warfare against the pitcher. The same thing is true in a football game. The players take off their helmets when they come to the sideline, but put them back on when they go back on the field. That is essentially the distinction that the apostle Paul is communicating. There are some long-range elements of preparation and some for immediate readiness as the battle ensues.

God doubly protects His children. It would have been enough protection to have confidence in God's power by wearing the right shoes, the breastplate of righteousness, and the belt of commitment. But God gives us a double protection. Colossians 3:3 says, "Your life is hidden with Christ in God." That would have been sufficient, but John 10:27-29 says that we are Christ's sheep. We are in His hand and the Father's hand, and no one can remove us. Both God and Christ hold onto the believer, securing and hiding us. The Christian soldier has a double protection from the enemy.

B. Describing the Shield of Faith

When the battle gets furious and the arrows start flying, the believer takes up the shield of faith. What is it used for? Ephesians 6:16 says, "With which ye shall be able to quench [extinguish] all the fiery darts of the wicked." The shield of faith is enough to protect you. In a sense, it is complete enough to be the only piece of armor you need.

1. Its enemy

   a) His character

   The fiery darts come from "the wicked." The Greek text should be translated, "the wicked one." He is Satan. "The wicked" is *ponēros* in the Greek. Which means, "the bad one, the vile one, the wretched one." Satan uses his demons to shoot the fiery darts, but we quench them with the shield of faith.

The Devil Is Real

The phrase "the evil one" reminds us that this battle is not against a philosophy; it's against a personal being. The *L.A. Times* reviewed a book by a man named Robert Jewett, who claims that people who talk about the second coming of Jesus Christ are misrepresenting the truth of the Bible (John Dart, "Author Disputes Apocalyptic Doomsayers" [28 May, 1979], sec. 1, p. 31). One of the things he implies is that the devil isn't real. That's not true. In Ephesians 6:11 Paul says that there is a devil. There's no question about his reality. He is the source of our warfare. We are not fighting an abstract impersonal thing. When you and I write letters to stop gay rights or abortion, we are not fighting some kind of philosophical, impersonal abstraction; we are fighting the devil and his demons. They actively and aggressively attack the truth and character of God and His people.

b) His weapons

What are the fiery darts? In the battles of Roman times, archers would put a cotton material on the tip of their arrows and soak it in pitch, which would burn slowly but was very hot. Before they shot the arrow, they would light it. When the arrow hit its target, the pitch would splatter and start little fires on the clothing of the soldier or on a wooden target.

What are Satan's fiery darts? They are seducing temptations. Satan fires shafts of impurity, selfishness, doubt, fear, disappointment, lust, greed, vanity, and covetousness. Those temptations are all part of the lust of the flesh, the lust of the eyes, and the pride of life (1 John 2:16). Satan literally bombards the believer with the fiery darts of seductive temptation to elicit ungodly, evil responses. The only defense we have at that point is the shield of faith. We live in a world where Satan often rains temptation on us. That's why we must have the shield of faith.

2. Its effectiveness

Why is faith a shield against temptation? How does faith parry the arrows and secure the victory?

a) The act of believing

To have faith is to believe God. That is the bottom line of the Christian faith—the bottom line of everything we believe, everything we hold to, and everything we have confidence in. The whole of Christianity is an act of believing that God "is, and that he is a rewarder of them that diligently seek him" (Heb. 11:6). We believe that He wrote the Bible, that Christ is God, that Christ died, rose, and is coming again. We know that by believing we can enter into His kingdom. That's why the Bible says that the just shall live by faith (Hab. 2:4; Rom. 1:17; Gal. 3:11; Heb. 10:38). When God says something that many times, you know it's important. Faith is our life—we believe God.

Christian Faith Is Not in Something

Everyone has faith in something. When you get in your car, you have faith it will get you where you're going without blowing up. I remember an ad in a magazine that pictured a monstrous earthmover. A man was standing next to it with his arms folded. The caption read, "I call her Faith because she can move mountains." I remember an article I read in *Reader's Digest* about a Kansas town that had problems with its water, which came out of a huge storage tank. They discovered that when the storage tank was drained to convert to another system, all kinds of dead animals were at the bottom. I'm sure cases of retroactive dysentery showed up! It's one thing to live by faith, but you had better be sure your faith is in the right thing.

Oliver Wendell Holmes said, "It is faith in something that makes life worth living." That's not true. A little leaguer told his mom, "I think we're going to lose the game today." She said, "No son, think positive!" He replied, "I'm positive we're going to lose the game today." Faith must be in something that's worth putting faith in. What is faith? Faith is believing God. Every fiery dart that Satan ever shoots is a lie. If you and I believe his lies, we're not believing God.

The Translation That Saved a Civilization

When missionary John Paton was translating the Scripture for the South Sea islanders, he was unable to find a word in their vocabulary for the concept of believing, trusting, or having faith. He had no idea how he would convey that to them. One day while he was in his hut translating, a native came running up the stairs into Paton's study and flopped in a chair, exhausted. He said to Paton, "It's so good to rest my whole weight in this chair." John Paton had his word: Faith is resting your whole weight on God. That word went into the translation of their New Testament and helped bring that civilization of natives to Christ. Believing is putting your whole weight on God. If God said it, then it's true, and we're to believe it.

    b)   The work of temptation

        (1) On Adam and Eve

           In the Garden of Eden, God created a perfect environment. He also created a perfect man and woman—perfect in the sense of sinlessness but not in the sense of proven perfection. So Satan, disguised as a serpent, said to Eve, "Hath God said?" (Gen. 3:1). Then he said, "God doesn't want you to know good and evil because you'll be like Him. He doesn't like competition. You can't trust Him because He has ulterior motives." Satan was tempting her to doubt God and believe him instead. Eve was a fool; she believed the devil. Since then, every temptation provides the chance to believe Satan and not God.

(2) On Christ

The account of Christ's temptation is found in Matthew 4:1-11 and Luke 4:1-13. Christ was led into the wilderness by the Spirit of God as He was being prepared for His ministry (Matt. 4:1). Jesus fasted for forty days and nights (v. 2). At the end of that time, Satan tempted Him to disbelieve God. The following was his approach:

(a) Temptation #1

Satan first asked Christ to turn stones into bread (v. 3). There's nothing wrong with doing that if you're the Son of God—it's not a moral issue. It's not a sin to eat bread. It's also not a sin to perform a miracle for God. But Satan was saying, "You've been in the wilderness with nothing to eat for forty days. Has God abandoned You? He said He would take care of You, sustain You, and replenish Your need. You're the Son of God; grab some satisfaction. You can't wait for God; He's forgotten You." Satan was tempting Christ to distrust God and take control of His destiny.

(b) Temptation #2

Then Satan said, "Didn't God promise to make You the Messiah? Didn't He promise that every knee would bow before You? Didn't He promise that You would be King and receive homage and worship? Come with me. We'll go to the top of the Temple and You can dive off it. Angels will protect You and the people will know You are the Messiah" (vv. 5-6).

123

(c) Temptation #3

Satan then said, "Didn't God tell You He would give You the kingdoms of the world? Come with me and I'll give them to You" (vv. 8-9). In other words, "Don't believe God; He doesn't keep His word or tell you the truth."

(3) On believers today

Satan tempts Christians to believe him. He will say, "I know the Bible says that you're not supposed to have sexual relationships outside of marriage, but it's fun." *Christianity Today* interviewed some Christians in an article entitled, "Sex and Singleness the Second Time Around" (Harold Ivan Smith [25 May, 1979]). One man they interviewed had had over fifty sexual involvements and wasn't married. He said, "Christ wants us to live abundant lives; to me that includes sex." Whom is he believing? He's not believing God; he's believing Satan. Every time you sin, you've believed Satan's lie. Someone will say, "I know the Bible says I should only marry a Christian. But I have a wonderful relationship with someone who isn't a Christian. We're all praying that the Lord will do a saving work. After all, the Lord is gracious." God says don't do it; Satan says do it. God says, "Don't read that dirty magazine, don't watch that dirty film, don't cheat on your income tax, don't claim something you don't have on your expense account." Satan says, "Do it. You'll get more money and you'll have more thrills." Whom do you believe? When you sin you believe Satan; when you obey you believe God.

c) The faith of obedience

The shield is your protection. When Christ was tempted, He essentially said, "I will believe God; begone Satan. God will feed Me, anoint Me as Messiah, and give Me the kingdoms of the world when He's ready. I will believe His terms, not yours." First John 5:10 says that if you doubt God, you make Him a liar. Is God a liar? Titus 1:2 says that God cannot lie. But every time you sin, you believe

Satan. You say, "I know I ought to give something to the Lord, but I want to buy this instead." We do what we want and shove God in a corner. But all we've done is cheat ourselves.

(1) God's promises

  (a) The resistance to obedience: unbelief

    God won't give you a stone when you ask Him for bread. He wants to open the windows of heaven and pour out so much blessing on you, you couldn't even contain it. He wants to give to you abundantly. He wants to bless you "with all spiritual blessings in the heavenly places" (Eph. 1:3). He wants "to do exceedingly abundantly above all that we ask or think" (Eph. 3:20). He wants to give you every good and perfect thing that "cometh down from the Father of lights, with whom is no variableness, neither shadow of turning" (James 1:17). He wants to bless you for as long as you live. If you believe He wants to do all that, then believe and obey Him so He can do so.

    Satan says, "Do it my way; you'll like it. It will fulfill you." But that's a lie. John 8:44 says that Satan "is a liar, and the father of [lies]." Whenever you sin, you are saying, "I don't believe God knows best; Satan knows best." Do you believe that? Philippians 4:19 says, "My God shall supply all your need according to his riches in glory by Christ Jesus." We say amen to that. But when we lose a job, we say, "God, what are You doing to me?" We think the Lord has forsaken us. We know the Bible says in effect, "I've never seen God's people begging bread" (Ps. 37:25). We know that Matthew 6:33 says, "Seek ye first the kingdom of God, and his righteousness, and all these things shall be added unto you." But we go through life seeking the things we need and pass by the kingdom of God. You can't say, "I believe God. I will live by faith," and then grab everything you can.

125

(b) The result of obedience: blessing
  i) Proverbs 8:34—"Blessed is the man who heareth me."
  ii) Jeremiah 15:16—Jeremiah lived in the midst of a society that didn't listen to God. Yet he said, "Thy words were found, and I did eat them, and thy word was unto me the joy and rejoicing of mine heart."
  iii) Psalm 119—From beginning to end this psalm declares how wonderful it is to obey the Word of God.
  iv) Revelation 1:3—"Blessed is he that readeth . . . and keep those things which are written in it."
  v) 1 John 1:4—"And these things write we unto you, that your joy may be full."

If you want abundant joy and blessing, obey the Word. If you want your heart to burn in you as it did for the two disciples on the road to Emmaus (Luke 24:32), then let the Word find root in your life. Satan says, "Don't believe God; do what you want." Every time you sin you believe the devil. That's stupid, but we keep doing it. I hate Satan so much, I don't want to give him the satisfaction of seeing me sin. And I don't want to forfeit the blessing of God.

(2) God's shield

The only way to quench the darts of Satan is to believe God.

(a) Romans 4:3—"Abraham believed God, and it was counted unto him for righteousness." Whom do you believe?

(b) 2 Corinthians 1:24—"By faith ye stand." The shield of faith causes us to stand.

(c) Proverbs 30:5-6—"Every word of God is pure; he is a shield unto those who put their trust in him. Add thou not unto his words, lest he reprove thee, and thou be found a liar." What God says is true. If you believe and obey His Word, it will be a shield. But if you don't, you will suffer. Satan says, "I

126

know God said that, but let me add this." No. God is a shield to those who put their trust in Him.

(d) Psalm 12:6—"The words of the Lord are pure words, like silver tested in a furnace of earth, purified seven times."

(e) Psalm 18:30—"As for God, his way is perfect; the word of the Lord is proved; he is a shield to all those who trust in him." As long as you believe God, your shield is up. If Satan lies and you believe it, then the shield comes down. Trust God in everything.

(f) 1 John 5:4—"This is the victory that overcometh the world, even our faith." We win by believing and trusting in God. You may have doubts and anxieties, and various struggles and trials, but as long as you believe in God's Word and power, you will be strengthened.

(g) 1 Peter 5:8-9—"Be sober, be vigilant, because your adversary, the devil, like a roaring lion walketh about, seeking whom he may devour; whom resist steadfast in the faith." You resist the devil by believing God.

3. Its empowerment

The shield of faith is the consistent application of what we believe about God to the issues of life. If you don't trust Him, then you don't know Him well enough. The more you know God—the more you know about the truth of His Word, and the more you meditate upon His person in your prayers—the more you will trust in Him. The more you trust God, the less likely you will be not to believe Him. What's most important is your relationship to God. If you love Him with all your heart, soul, mind, and strength, and believe He is who He claims to be, and that all His promises are true, you're not going to sin. You are going to be standing in the place of greatest blessing. Everyone wants to be blessed. God says, "I will bless you if you obey Me." If you follow Satan, you disbelieve God.

The more you know God, the more you will trust and believe Him.

a) Genesis 15:1—God said, "Fear not, Abram: I am thy shield."

b) Psalm 46:1—"God is our refuge and strength, a very present help in trouble."

c) Proverbs 18:10—"The name of the Lord is a strong tower; the righteous runneth into it, and is safe.

d) Psalm 84:11—"For the Lord God is a sun and a shield."

God is on your side. He wants to bless you and give you victory over Satan. But you have to believe Him and obey His Word.

We are ready for the battle when we're wearing the belt of commitment, the breastplate of righteousness, and the shoes of confidence that God is on our side. When the battle begins, we grab the shield of faith to parry the fiery darts of temptation by trusting God implicitly. There is no reason to lose the battle, because ultimately the victory is ours. Romans 8:37 says, "We are more than conquerors." If we put the armor on, we will win.

Focusing on the Facts

1. Explain the positional victory that the Christian has in Christ. Support your explanation with Scripture (see p. 114).
2. According to 2 Chronicles 20:22-30, how did the people of Israel become superconquerors (see p. 115)?
3. What were the two kinds of shields that Roman soldiers used in battle? Describe each one (see pp. 117-18).
4. Describe the strategy the Romans used during a battle (see p. 118).
5. Why do the final three pieces of armor provide a double protection from the enemy? What is the purpose of the first three pieces of armor (see pp. 119-20)?
6. What is the shield of faith used for (Eph. 6:16; see p. 120)?
7. Define "the wicked" (see p. 120).
8. What was the purpose of fiery darts during a battle (see p. 120)?
9. What are the fiery darts of Satan (see p. 121)?
10. What does faith mean (see p. 121)?
11. How did Satan tempt Eve in the Garden of Eden? What did Eve do (Gen. 3:1-5; see p. 122-23)?
12. Describe the ways Satan tempted Christ in the wilderness (Matt. 4:1-11; see pp. 123-24).
13. How does Satan tempt believers today (see p. 124)?
14. What does God want to do for all who obey Him (see p. 126)?

15. Give some Scripture verses that show the result of obedience (see p. 126).
16. What is the only way the believer can quench the darts of Satan (see p. 126)?
17. What is one advantage to having an intimate knowledge of God (see pp. 127-28)?

Pondering the Principles

1. Read Romans 8:31-39. Meditate on the victory you have in Christ. Since you are more than a conqueror by the fact of your salvation, what effect should that have on your daily living? Does that make you want to fight harder in your daily battles, or do you think you don't need to fight since you have won the war? Remember, if you don't fight the battles today, you won't experience the victory today. You'll only experience defeat. Start fighting today!
2. How do you respond to each of the following darts of Satan: impurity, selfishness, doubt, fear, disappointment, lust, greed, vanity, and covetousness? How would you use the shield of faith to defend yourself against each of those attacks? Record your answers and prepare to use them for the next attack.
3. What is your first reaction when you realize that God wants to bless you if you obey Him? Does that make you want to obey Him more or less? In reality, what do you usually do? The hardest thing for most Christians is to put their godly desires into action. If you are having trouble obeying God, perhaps you don't know Him well enough. Whom would you have more of a tendency to obey: a friend or a stranger? Plan to spend more time with God each day so that you might get to know Him better.

8
The Believer's Armor—
Part 5

Outline

Introduction
A. The Christian's Conflict
B. The Christian's Victory
   1. Ephesians 3:20-21
   2. Ephesians 4:1
   3. Ephesians 5:18

Review
I. The Belt of Truthfulness
II. The Breastplate of Righteousness
III. The Shoes of the Gospel of Peace
IV. The Shield of Faith

Lesson
V. The Helmet of Salvation
   A. The Soldier's Helmet
   B. The Saint's Salvation
      1. The theology of salvation
         a) The past aspect—freedom from the penalty of sin
         b) The present aspect—freedom from the power of sin
         c) The future aspect—freedom from the presence of sin
      2. The testimony of Scripture
         a) Romans 8:22-24
         b) Galatians 5:5
         c) 1 Peter 1:3-6
         d) 1 Thessalonians 5:8-9
   C. Satan's Sword
      1. Discouragement
         a) A representative illustration
            (1) The remarkable review
            (2) The revengeful resistance

   (3) The running retreat
   (4) The restoring rest
   (5) The reassuring revelation
  b) A relentless battle
  c) A renewed encouragement
   (1) For Old Testament saints
    (*a*) Jeremiah
    (*b*) Job
   (2) For the believer
   (3) For Timothy
  d) A restored strength

Introduction

In Ephesians 6:13-17 Paul represents the resources for gaining victory in the Christian life against Satan and his demons. We need to be ready for the conflict because it will not be easy. We will be withstood, sidetracked, attacked, and thwarted by Satan on every side.

A. The Christian's Conflict

 The Bible discusses the Christian's conflict in three dimensions:

 1. Between the flesh and the Spirit (Gal. 5:16-26)
 2. Between the Christian and the world (John 15:18-27)
 3. Between the believer and demons (Eph. 6:10-17)

  This last conflict cannot be separated from the other two because demons will work through the world and the flesh. How can a believer have a victory in his life with the tremendous amount of opposition he faces from the wiles of the devil (v. 11) and from principalities, powers, rulers, and spiritual wickedness (v. 12)?

B. The Christian's Victory

 How can we gain the victory in this sophisticated warfare? Let me give you some basics.

 1. Ephesians 3:20-21—Verse 20 sums up the first three chapters: "Now unto him who is able to do exceedingly abundantly above all that we ask or think, according to the power that worketh in us." We have the power to glorify God (v. 21).
 2. Ephesians 4:1—Since the power is available to glorify God, we are to "walk worthy."

3. Ephesians 5:18—How do we tap the power to walk worthy? "And be not drunk with wine, in which is excess [Gk., *asōtia*], but be filled with the Spirit." We have the necessary resources. That makes us responsible to walk in the right way. We tap the resource through the filling of the Spirit. Our Lord said, "Ye shall receive power, after the Holy Spirit is come upon you" (Acts 1:8). When we tap that power, we will be victorious.

There is nothing to fear. The power is available, the command is given, and the Spirit of God enables us to tap the power. We can go into the army and directly into the war with victory at hand. But that doesn't mean the battle is going to be easy; it is relentless. Some of us are winning and some of us are losing. Perhaps some of you are in a stalemate. But as long as you live in this world, the battle will go on. As you grow in Christ by feeding on the Word, you will begin to win more often than you lose. But everyone experiences some victories and some defeats.

A Letter from the Battlefield

I received a letter from a radio listener to our program in Boston. He said, "Dear John MacArthur: Your ministry has been of great significance to me and I wanted to take this opportunity to thank you personally as well as express my desire to lend you my financial support. May God continue to bless and multiply your spiritual growth and outreach everywhere, including here in the Boston area, where we listen on WEZE. I am a young man of twenty-three years and came to Jesus Christ at the age of nineteen. In that time I have grown in the Word, staggered, fallen down, been crushed, been convinced by a neurotic legalist that I was demon-possessed, been arrested for driving under the influence of alcohol, gotten a woman friend pregnant, received professional Christian counseling from a licensed psychologist, and begun to regain my spiritual senses. Everything, as you can see, has been just fine.

"Please send me some ammunition and prayer support. The battle lines are drawn, the trenches are being dug, and I am not going to be one of those caught shame-faced when our Commanding Officer returns. When the record is being reviewed, I want it written that the soldier in question, after repeatedly disobeying orders and going AWOL during wartime alert, donned his armor, reported back to his Commanding Officer, fought courageously and fearlessly without batting an eye, and hit the enemy with everything he could get his hands on and inflicted heavy damage in strategic areas to the credit of his patient, forgiving Commanding Officer. Amen.

"Remember me in your prayers, please. Sincerely, (with the 'sin covered') C.T." He's been in the battle! So have you, and so have I. Being victorious in the battle is a matter of putting on the armor.

Review

I. THE BELT OF TRUTHFULNESS (v. 14a; see p. 65)

Ephesians 6:14 says, "Stand, therefore, having your loins girded about with truth." The apostle Paul talking about the attitude of truthfulness—commitment without hypocrisy. You are to gird up your loins, an old Jewish expression meaning readiness or anticipation. A soldier must be ready for battle. He must make a commitment. If we're going to win, we need to be committed to victory from the beginning.

II. THE BREASTPLATE OF RIGHTEOUSNESS (v. 14b; see p. 79)

The Christian arms himself with purity, holiness, and practical righteousness. Imputed righteousness from Christ is the basis of our own righteousness. But we must maintain a pure life or Satan will hurt us in the vital areas.

III. THE SHOES OF THE GOSPEL OF PEACE (v. 15; see p. 103)

The gospel of peace is the good news that we are at peace with God. We were once enemies fighting against God, but we who believe the gospel have made peace with Him. Romans 5:1 says, "Therefore, being justified by faith, we have peace with God." The shoes allow us to stand firm against Satan because God is on our side. We can resist anything because His resources are available.

These three pieces of armor are connected to the verb "having," indicating they are to be worn constantly. But when the battle gets hot, you pick up the remaining pieces. The verb changes from "having" to "taking" in verses 16-17. The soldier who had his belt, breastplate, and shoes securely on would then take his helmet, shield and sword.

IV. THE SHIELD OF FAITH (v. 16; see p. 117)

Verse 16 says we are to take "the shield of faith, with which [we] shall be able to quench all the fiery darts of the wicked." Satan shoots arrows of temptation. The only way we can quench them is with our faith. Whenever you sin, you have believed the devil's lie. But as long as you believe God's Word, you will not believe Satan. God says, "Do what I tell you and you'll be blessed." Satan says, "Do this and you'll like it. God won't care. He won't chasten you." Whom do you believe? When you believe Satan, you sin; when you believe God, you don't.

Lesson

V. THE HELMET OF SALVATION (v. 17a)

A. The Soldier's Helmet

A Roman soldier wouldn't go to battle without a helmet. That would be foolish. Helmets were made out of two things: leather, with some patches of metal on it, or solid cast metal. The helmet protected the head from arrows, but its primary function was to ward off blows from a broadsword. There were two swords carried in battle: the *machaira*, the dagger mentioned in verse 17, and the broadsword, which was from three- to four-feet long. It had a massive handle that was held with both hands like a baseball bat. The soldier lifted it over his head and brought it down on his opponent's head. The broadsword was a tremendous weapon. It dealt such a crushing blow to the skull a helmet was necessary to deflect it. I read in a newspaper that at an archaeological dig, a skeleton was discovered with a cleavage right through the skull. It is assumed that it had been made by someone who attacked the person with a broadsword.

B. The Saint's Salvation

The helmet of salvation does not refer to being saved. Paul is not saying that after fighting Satan by donning the breastplate of righteousness, the shoes of the gospel of peace, and the shield of faith, you should get saved. That's already happened. You're not in the army unless you're a believer. If you're fighting Satan, you have to be on God's side (Matt. 12:30). If you're not for Him, you're against Him. The helmet of salvation is not about becoming saved. Paul had already discussed the issue of salvation in Ephesians 2:8-9: "For by grace are ye saved through faith; and that not of yourselves,

135

it is the gift of God—not of works, lest any man should boast." You wouldn't be in the army if you weren't a believer. Satan wouldn't attack you if you weren't a believer. The helmet of salvation is not indicating that you need to be saved. It is indicating something else.

1. The theology of salvation

Many people are confused about eternal security. I am frequently asked, "Do you believe in the concept of once saved, always saved?" People are concerned about that. They commit sin and then feel guilty, often saying, "I don't know if I'm saved anymore." I have asked certain young people, "Have you given your life to Christ?" A frequent response is: "Yes, many times. And just to be sure, I did it again today." How can we understand the security of the believer? By understanding the meaning of salvation.

There are three aspects to salvation: past, present, and future.

a) The past aspect—freedom from the penalty of sin

If you were to ask me, "Are you a Christian? Have you been saved?" I would say yes. Years ago I confessed Jesus Christ and invited Him into my life. At that moment my sins were placed on Him on the cross and my penalty for those sins was paid—I died to sin. Paul said, "I am crucified with Christ: nevertheless I live" (Gal. 2:20). In Romans 6 Paul says that if you died once, you don't need to die again. When did you die? You died when you put your faith in Christ. You were crucified with Him, the penalty was paid, sin was dealt with, and there's no more penalty to pay. Romans 8:1 says, "There is, therefore, now no condemnation to them who are in Christ Jesus."

b) The present aspect—freedom from the power of sin

Sin no longer has dominion over you. Why? First John 1:9 says, "He is faithful and just to forgive us our sins, and to cleanse us from all unrighteousness." Not one sin can be put against your account. Romans 8:33 says, "Who shall lay any thing to the charge of God's elect?" No one. He's forgiven you all your trespasses for His name's sake. He keeps on purifying and purging. Jesus said to Peter that he needed to take a bath once, and then he only had to wash his feet the rest of his life (John 13:10). The Lord bathes you at salvation and cleans your feet day-by-day. That's the present aspect of salvation. Romans 5:10 says, "For if, when we were enemies, we were reconciled to God by the death of his Son, much more, being reconciled, we shall be saved by his life." Christ lives to make intercession for us (Heb. 7:25). We continually experience salvation as He constantly cleanses us.

c) The future aspect—freedom from the presence of sin

A day is coming when there will be no more sin. The book of Revelation says there will be no more death (Rev. 21:4). Romans 6:23 says, "For the wages of sin is death." First John 3:2 says, "We shall be like him; for we shall see him as he is." Christ is sinless, spotless, and without flaw or blemish. A day is coming when we will be saved from the presence of sin.

Salvation has happened—that's justification; it is happening—that's sanctification; and it will happen—that's glorification. Romans 8:30 says, "Whom he justified, them he also glorified." Salvation is past, present, and future. If salvation is past, it is accomplished. If it is also present, then you can't lose it because it is continuing. And if it is guaranteed in the future, then you are absolutely secure. That is the heart and soul of the meaning of salvation.

2. The testimony of Scripture

a) Romans 8:22-24—Here Paul is talking about the curse. Sin affected creation by making it subject to vanity, but there is still hope for something different. The world will someday be perfect, but not until Jesus comes. It won't get perfect by man's efforts. That's why hope is a very important part of Christian experience. In verse 22 Paul says, "For we know that the whole creation groaneth and travaileth in pain together until now." The world itself knows that something is desperately wrong. The created order is actually chaotic. Verse 23 says, "And not only they, but ourselves also [we know things aren't the way God intended them to be], who have the first fruits of the Spirit, even we ourselves groan within ourselves, waiting for the adoption, that is, the redemption of our body." Our souls have been saved—and are

137

being saved. Someday our bodies will be saved along with our souls. That will result in absolute holiness. That's why verse 24 says, "We are saved [in] hope."

Would You Run in a Race Without a Finish Line?

If someone said to me, "The salvation that you now have is all there is. There's no future aspect to salvation," I would say, "Do you mean I have to fight the flesh the rest of my life throughout eternity? Do you mean I will always have to fight the devil and live with human weaknesses?" That would make me cry with Paul, "Oh, wretched man that I am! Who shall deliver me from the body of this death?" (Rom. 7:24). If there were no future aspect to salvation, I would say that salvation is incomplete. If all the Lord does is aid me in the struggle, but holds no hope for the end of the struggle, then salvation never reaches fruition. But that isn't all there is to salvation; there is a future element that gives us the hope of reaching the point where there will be no sin.

Living without hope would be like running a race without a finish line. It would be ridiculous for someone to say, "Start running for the rest of your life. There's no finish, but give everything you have." Can you imagine God saying that? Revelation 14:13 says that when the saints die, they rest from their labors. There will be a finish line in the future.

b) Galatians 5:5—"For we [believers] through the Spirit wait for the hope of righteousness by faith." Paul is not talking about the past or present element of salvation, but about the fullness of it. We are waiting in hope. We are holding onto the hope that someday the battle will be over and we won't have to struggle with sin, the flesh, the devil, the world, and demons. Someday we will know the hope of full righteousness.

c) 1 Peter 1:3-6—"Blessed be the God and Father of our Lord Jesus Christ, who, according to his abundant mercy, hath begotten us again unto a living hope by the resurrection of Jesus Christ from the dead, to an inheritance incorruptible, and undefiled, and that fadeth not away, reserved in heaven for you, who are kept by the power of God through faith unto salvation ready

138

to be revealed in the last time" (vv. 3-5). There is a final element of salvation—the consummation of our living hope—when we go to heaven and receive the inheritance that God has for us. Therefore, we don't mind "a season . . . [of] heaviness through manifold trials" (v. 6). We don't mind a little painful effort when there is a finish line. God has not just given us a past salvation and present salvation, He has also given us tremendous hope for a future salvation. There is an end—a finish line. The helmet of salvation is our hope of ultimate salvation.

d) 1 Thessalonians 5:8-9—The night is Satan's dominion. We are of the day; we are sons of light in God's kingdom. Paul says, "But let us, who are of the day, be sober, putting on the breastplate of faith and love, and, for an helmet, the hope of salvation. For God hath not appointed us to wrath but to obtain salvation" (vv. 8-9). There still is an element of salvation to obtain. God has appointed it to us. That is represented by the helmet of salvation. The writer of Hebrews says our hope is the anchor of the soul (Heb. 6:19). I couldn't fight if I didn't know there was a finish line.

C. Satan's Sword

The Roman soldier had to defend himself against a broadsword. Satan's broadsword has two sides to it: discouragement and doubt. Satan wants to belt you in the head with discouragement and doubt. His attacks of discouragement might go like this: "You sure are giving a lot and not getting much in return. You're circumscribing your life to a certain standard and setting yourself apart from the world. But what happens? You just lost your job! Some blessing! You've been reading your Bible every day, but your wife is as cranky as she was before you bought it, and it hasn't had any effect on her. What is God doing in your life? You've been going to church for years, but look at your kids. They don't respect you today anymore than they ever did." That would discourage anyone. You might have been teaching a class for a long time, yet wonder if anyone is getting anything out of it. That could discourage you.

Satan also wants to hit you in the head with doubt: "How do

you know you're a Christian? Are you sure you're saved? You certainly don't deserve to be; look what you just did! Do you think that's what a Christian does?" Many people suffer from doubt and discouragement, but the helmet of salvation is our protection.

1. Discouragement

   a) A representative illustration

      (1) The remarkable review

          First Kings 19 records a great story about Elijah. he had just experienced great victory. He slaughtered four hundred and fifty priests of Baal (1 Kings 18:22, 40). Can you imagine killing the leading false prophets of the day in the name of the Lord? You would have a right to say, "Lord, this was a good day: We just eliminated people who represented the kingdom of darkness!" God sent fire down from heaven, burned up the sacrifice and the altar, and licked up the water that had been poured around the altar (1 Kings 18:38). Elijah was triumphant.

      (2) The revengeful resistance

          First Kings 19:1-2 says, "And Ahab told Jezebel all that Elijah had done, and how he had slain all the prophets with the sword. Then Jezebel sent a messenger unto Elijah, saying, So let the gods do to me, and more also, if I make not thy life as the life of one of them by tomorrow about this time." Jezebel was a Baal worshiper. For doing what he did to the priests, she was going to kill him by the next day or die trying. Elijah could have said, "Lord, I just did You a big favor. Four hundred and fifty priests of Baal have been eliminated. Then You send Jezebel after me the next day. How about a little rest?" If Elijah could handle four hundred and fifty priests of Baal, you would think one woman wouldn't shake him.

      (3) The running retreat

          Elijah decided the only thing to do was run. Now God never meant for eighty-year-old prophets to be running to faraway places, but he ran "for his life, and came to Beersheba, which belongeth to Judah, and left his servant there. But he himself went a day's journey into the wilderness, and came and sat under a juniper tree. And he requested for himself that he might die, and said, It is enough! Now, O Lord take away my life" (vv. 3-4). That's what I call discouragement! He wanted to die.

(4) The restoring rest

The narrative continues; "And as he lay and slept under a juniper tree, behold, an angel touched him, and said unto him, Arise and eat. And he looked, and, behold, there was a cake baked on the coals, and a cruse of water at his head. And he did eat and drink, and lay down again. And the angel of the Lord came again the second time, and touched him, and said, Arise and eat, because the journey is too great for thee. And he arose, and did eat and drink, and went in the strength of that food forty days and forty nights unto Horeb, the mount of God" (vv. 5-8).

(5) The reassuring revelation

Elijah had no reason to be discouraged, so God sent him to Mount Horeb to confer with him. The Lord spoke in a still, small voice (v. 12). Elijah claimed he was the only faithful person the Lord had remaining (v. 14). But the Lord said that He had seven thousand other faithful servants beside Elijah (v. 18).

It's easy to become discouraged. I can vouch for that. Even at the moment of some of your greatest triumphs, reality can be stark and shocking.

b) A relentless battle

(1) Ephesians 3:13—Paul said, "Wherefore, I desire that ye faint not at my tribulations." Some people become discouraged over the trouble of others. It is not always one's own troubles that bring discouragement.

(2) Galatians 6:9—"Let us not be weary in well doing; for in due season we shall reap, if we faint not." It is easy to become weary. I sometimes think, "Lord, do I have to preach another sermon on Sunday? Do I have to study another day?" You might think, "Do I have to disciple another

person? Can't I have a few days off from reading my Bible? I can't handle that Sunday school class another Sunday! Lord, I don't have to talk to my neighbor another time, do I? Lord, You know I've been fighting this same temptation a long time; I'm getting tired." It is easy to become discouraged. Nineteenth-century writer Arthur H. Clough expressed that feeling in these words:

> Say not the struggle naught availeth,
> The labor and the words are vain,
> The enemy faints not, nor faileth,
> And as things have been, they remain.

Have you noticed that you get tired but the enemy doesn't? Nineteenth-century English poet Matthew Arnold wrote,

> For now in blood and battle was my youth,
> And full of blood and battles is my age;
> And I shall never end this life of blood!

The battle never stops because we fight the foe all our lives.

(3) 2 Timothy 4:7—The apostle Paul came to the end of his life and said, "I have fought a good fight, I have finished my course, I have kept the faith."

(4) Acts 20:24—Paul was told that if he went to Jerusalem, he would be imprisoned in chains. But he said, "None of these things move me, neither count I my life dear unto myself, so that I might finish my course with joy, and the ministry, which I have received of the Lord Jesus."

(5) Revelation 2:3—The Lord extolled the virtues of the Ephesian church when he said, "[Thou] hast borne, and hast patience, and for my name's sake hast labored, and hast not fainted."

(6) Leviticus 26—God essentially told Israel, "If you keep My statutes and obey My ordinances, I will bless your lives, your land, and your children" (vv. 3-13). But in verses 14-39 He says in effect, "But if you turn from My statutes and commandments, I will bring corruption, pain, and sorrow on you." So be obedient.

c) A renewed encouragement

Perhaps you get discouraged because you have an unsaved husband, and he never wants to change. Maybe you have a child who is resistant to all your efforts. Maybe you have a friend you've tried to witness to. Maybe you don't get the thanks you ought to for your ministry. Perhaps you have a physical infirmity that causes you to grow tired of struggling. Those things can cause you to lose sight of the future aspect of salvation. Romans 13:11 says, "Our salvation [is] nearer than when we believed." We're getting close to the finish line; don't quit now.

The writer of Hebrews addresses those who had acknowledged the truth of Christ only to go back to where they had been. So he says, "Don't turn around and fall back into perdition (Heb. 10:39); let us go on to perfection" (Heb. 12:2).

(1) For Old Testament saints

(a) Jeremiah

The Lord told Jeremiah that he was His prophet. He essentially said, "I want you to spend your life preaching for Me. Preach the message with all your energy. However, no one will ever listen to you" (Jer. 1:5-8). Jeremiah preached all alone. Nevertheless he said, "Thy words were found, and I did eat them, and thy word was unto me the joy and rejoicing of mine heart" (Jer. 15:16).

(b) Job

The Lord stripped Job as naked as any man has ever been stripped. He took away everything he ever owned or loved. Yet Job said, "Though he slay me, yet will I trust in him" (Job 13:15). When the Lord revealed Himself, Job said, "I have heard of thee by the hearing of the ear, but now mine eye seeth thee. Wherefore I abhor myself, and repent in dust and ashes" (Job 42:5-6).

Don't let Satan hit you with discouragement. In Luke 18:1 Jesus says, "Men ought always to pray, and not to faint." When you see yourself fainting, start praying.

If You Work Long Enough

Two hundred years ago in England, a man by the name of Reverend William Davy toward the end of his life started to write a systematic theology encompassing the entire Bible. He spent twelve years doing it. When he was done, it covered twenty-six volumes. When he was finished with his work, he couldn't find anyone who would set the type, so he did it himself. He printed forty copies of the first three hundred pages and fourteen copies of the remaining volumes. There were only fourteen copies of his labor of twelve years. He was an obscure man. There are now no copies of his theology that I know of. He died in poverty and obscurity, though I'm sure he died with a great knowledge of God. He wrote a twenty-six volume theology that probably no one ever heard of, but he pursued the knowledge of God and stuck with it.

A story is told about a little girl in London who was standing on a sidewalk when a coal truck dumped a ton of coal in front of her house. She picked up a little shovel in the cellar, opened the cellar door, walked out to the pile of coal, got a little shovelful of coal, and walked back down the cellar stairs. A man who lived next door watched her for a while. After she had the third shovelful, he said to her, "My dear, you'll never get all that coal in the cellar." She replied brightly, "I will, sir, if I work long enough." The test of anyone's character is what it takes to stop them. Many people hit the first line of defense and bail out. But there are those who make a difference in the world because they go right through the line of opposition. You can do that if you work long enough. Don't be discouraged.

(2) For the believer

You have not suffered to the point of being crucified (Heb. 12:4). Satan will discourage you every way he can. He will tell you that you're not getting any results from your labors. He will say, "No one listens to you or praises you for what you faithfully do. Who will know if you fall to sin? Don't worry about the battle; give in a little. Relax." But the helmet of salvation protects me from fainting and from giving up. Why? Because I have a hope that there is a light at the end of the tunnel. Some day I'm going to burst into that glorious light in the presence of Jesus Christ. I don't want to stand in front of my Commanding Officer with shame on my face because I quit in the middle of the battle. I want to be able to say, "Lord, I may be bruised and bleeding, but I'm here. I fought all the way."

My grandfather died from cancer. As he lay on his deathbed, he looked up at my father and said, "I have just one request, Jack, and that is to preach one more sermon." My dad took the sermon he prepared but never preached, printed it, and passed it out to the church. In a way he did preach one more sermon. He was fighting right down to the wire. In Revelation 2 and 3 Christ continually says He will give something to those who overcome. God reserves special things for the overcomer.

(3) For Timothy

What discouraged Timothy? Many things. For one, he was young and tempted by youthful lusts (2 Tim. 2:22). Also, many people were saying that he was too young to know anything. They were despising his youth (1 Tim. 4:12). He became so discouraged that his stomach was upset. Paul told him to take a little wine for his stomach's sake (1 Tim. 5:23). He was also embarrassed because Paul always seemed to be in jail (2 Tim. 1:8). There were also some false teachers who came to Ephesus teaching sophisticated error. Timothy didn't know if he could handle them. They were discussing philosophies, vain deceits, and genealogies (1 Tim. 1:4-7). Timothy was drowning in a sea of discouragement. So the apostle Paul wrote to him saying, "Stir up the gift of God, which is in thee by the putting on of my hands. For God hath not given us the spirit of fear, but of power, and of love, and of a sound mind" (2 Tim. 1:6-7). Then Paul said, "Be strong in the grace that is in Christ Jesus" (2 Tim. 2:1).

Peter said, essentially the same kind of thing to the saints who were enduring persecution: "If you suffer for doing good, you are blessed; and if you suffer, commit your souls to the faithful Creator" (1 Pet. 4:14, 19).

d) A restored strength

You say, "But sometimes I get weary." When that happens to me, I often will think of Isaiah 40:29: "He giveth power to the faint; and to those who have no might he increaseth strength." Isn't that great? Just when you reach the place where you're about to faint, He gives you power. When you're ready to say, "Lord, I don't have any strength left," that's when He infuses you with His strength. Then Isaiah says, "Even the youths shall faint and be weary, and the young men shall utterly fall, but they that wait upon the Lord shall renew their strength; they shall mount up with wings like eagles; they shall run, and not be weary; and they shall walk, and not faint" (vv. 30-31). The eagle soars above most other birds. That is an illustration of what happens to a believer in his weakness: when he is infused with the strength of God, he soars above the rest.

There's no reason to be discouraged. The helmet of salvation lets you know that a great day of victory is coming. If you remain faithful, there will be a marvelous reward. Salvation is past and present, but it is also future. Don't let Satan discourage you. Don't let him rob you of the anticipation of that thrill. Don't let him take away the hope that makes you committed. In 1 John 3:3 John says, "Every man that hath this hope in him purifieth himself." Knowing that Jesus is coming and that salvation will ultimately be fulfilled purifies your life because you know you will see Him face-to-face.

Focusing on the Facts

1. What are the three dimensions of the Christian's conflict (see p. 132)?
2. Give some verses that show how we can gain victory over Satan (see pp. 132-33).
3. What purpose did the Roman soldier's helmet serve (see p. 135)?
4. Explain why the helmet of salvation does not refer to being saved (see p. 135).
5. What are the three aspects of salvation? What kind of freedom does each one provide (see pp. 136-37)?
6. Discuss the concept of dying to sin (see p. 136).

7. How does justification, sanctification, and glorification correspond to the three aspects of salvation (see p. 137)?
8. How did sin affect creation? Why is hope an important part of the Christian experience (Rom. 8:22-24; see p. 137)?
9. Why can living without hope be compared to running a race with no finish line (see p. 138)?
10. According to Hebrews 6:19, what is the anchor of the soul (see p. 139)?
11. What are the two sides of Satan's broadsword (see p. 139)?
12. What was the great victory that Elijah experienced in 1 Kings 18:40? What did Jezebel plan to do to Elijah (1 Kings 19:2; see p. 140)?
13. What was Elijah's reaction to Jezebel? How did the Lord respond to Elijah's actions (1 Kings 19:3-18; see p. 140)?
14. Give some verses that show how relentless the Christian battle is (see pp. 141-42).
15. Despite their trials, how did both Job and Jeremiah regard the Lord (see p. 143)?
16. How does the helmet of salvation protect you from fainting and giving up (see p. 144)?
17. What were some of the things that were discouraging Timothy? How did Paul encourage Timothy (see p. 145)?
18. What is a good verse to combat weariness in your battle with Satan (see p. 146)?

Pondering the Principles

1. When your battle record is reviewed by Jesus Christ, your Commanding Officer, what would you want it to say? Could it read that way today? If not, why? What attitudes or behavior do you have to change for the record to be revised?
2. Look up the following verses: John 5:26; 10:28-29; 14:19; Romans 8:34-39; Colossians 3:3-4; Revelation 1:18. List as many securities as you can. What are the chances of losing your salvation? As a result of knowing how secure you are, what kinds of changes do you need to make to bring God the most glory? Prayerfully consider what steps you should take to implement those changes.
3. What are some of the ways that Satan has tried to discourage you? How is he trying to discourage you today? How would you use the helmet of salvation to defend yourself against his attacks? How would you use what you have learned to encourage someone else who faces discouragement?
4. As a reminder for the times when you grow weary of the battle,

memorize Isaiah 40:31: "Those who wait for the Lord will gain new strength; they will mount up with wings like eagles, they will run and not get tired, they will walk and not become weary" (NASB).

9
The Believer's Armor— Part 6

Outline

Introduction
A. The Biblical Issue
    1. The proponents of surrendering
    2. The problem with surrendering
        a) The implication
        b) The illustration
B. The Biblical Approach
C. The Biblical Balance
    1. 2 Peter 1:3-7
        a) God's part
        b) Man's part
    2. Romans 6:12, 8:13
    3. Philippians 2:12-13
    4. Colossians 1:29
    5. 2 Corinthians 6:4-7

Review
  I. The Belt of Truthfulness
 II. The Breastplate of Righteousness
III. The Shoes of the Gospel of Peace
IV. The Shield of Faith
 V. The Helmet of Salvation
    A. The Soldier's Helmet
    B. The Saint's Salvation
        1. The theology of salvation
        2. The testimony of Scripture
    C. Satan's Sword
        1. Discouragement
            a) A representative illustration
            b) A relentless battle
            c) A renewed encouragement

Lesson
  d) A remembered hope
  e) A resurrection future
      (1) 1 Corinthians 15:32
      (2) 2 Corinthians 4:6-11, 14
  2. Doubt
      a) The false doctrine of eternal insecurity
          (1) Satan's ploy
          (2) Satan's purpose
      b) The true doctrine of eternal security
          (1) Security in the Trinity
              (a) God's gifts to Christ
              (b) God's will for Christ
          (2) Strands in the rope of security
          (3) Survival in the days of apostasy
              (a) A description of apostates
              (b) A description of the remnant
                  i) Jude 1
                  ii) Jude 24-25

Introduction

In our examination of the believer's warfare and his resources for victory, we have discussed the subject of commitment and dedication. We have said that we need to be obedient to fulfill God's will in our lives. We have looked at the matter of self-discipline, self-control, and conforming to the standards of Christ. We are to be soldiers, giving our best for His sake. That introduces another perspective of Christian living: Some people believe that all our effort and discipline is not what God wants. I want to respond to that perspective.

  A. The Biblical Issue

      1. The proponents of surrendering

          There is a statement in the Old Testament made in reference to King Jehoshaphat: "The battle is not yours, but God's" (2 Chron. 20:15). That verse has become a byword for a group of people referred to as *Quietists*. They say that the way to live the Christian life is not through self-discipline and commitment but through surrender.

          You may have been exposed to the concept of "Let go and let God." There is a song called "Let Go and Let God Have His Wonderful Way." There is a lot of discussion on the subject of yielding and abiding in Christ. People say, "Hand everything over to the Lord." There is a contemporary song titled "Turn It all Over to Jesus." People say, "Stop struggling and striving. Instead, yield and completely surrender." When I was young I remember hearing that frequently at camps and conferences. At one college I attended, there were constant altar calls. Students were forever going up to surrender themselves to God. Many of us were willing to surrender; we just weren't sure how to do that. It always seemed that after surrendering with tears, three days later we would sin. Then we would say, "We surrendered, Lord; whose fault is this?"

There are people who use the concept of abiding in Christ (John 15:4) to refer to surrendering and yielding, not to being saved. Maybe you're one of the people who went up aisles all your childhood years trying to get surrendered. That's not uncommon for many people. "Let go and let God" basically means to flake out and do nothing.

2. The problem with surrendering

   a) The implication

   Charles Trumbull, who used to defend this system, said that when we are fully surrendered, we don't even experience temptation because it is defeated by Christ before it has time to draw us into a fight (*Victory in Christ* [Philadelphia: Sunday School Times, 1959], pp. 5-8). If that's true, when you sin, whose fault is it? It must be Christ's fault, according to that train of thought, but that could not be true.

   b) The illustration

   The concept of surrender is aptly illustrated in *The Christian's Secret of a Happy Life* by Hannah Whitall Smith. She says, "What can be said about man's part in this great work but that he must continually surrender himself and continually trust? But when we come to God's side of the question, what is there that may not be said as to the manifold and wonderful ways, in which He accomplishes the work entrusted to Him? It is here that the growing comes in. The lump of clay could never grow into a beautiful vessel if it stayed in the clay pit for thousands of years; but when it is put into the hands of a skilful potter it grows rapidly, under his fashioning, into the vessel he intends it to be. And in the same way the soul, abandoned to the working of the Heavenly Potter, is made into a vessel unto honour, sanctified, and meet for the Master's use" ([Old Tappan, N.J.: Revell, 1952], p. 32). That sounds good, but if you are nothing but a piece of clay in the Potter's hand, who is making you into what He wants you to be? Why do you still sin? Does the clay suddenly hop out of the Potter's hand and then do what it wants? Hannah Whitall Smith portrays the Christian as a piece of soft clay, but when he sins, that means the clay has jumped out of the Potter's hand and is doing what it wants. There is more to the Christian life than that.

B. The Biblical Approach

The Bible doesn't teach that all you have to do is surrender. But there are many Christians who have tried. We must depend on God's energy, power, and strength, but it is unbiblical to think all we have to do is sit. The Bible teaches commitment and self-discipline in the Christian life by subjecting your flesh to the strength of God.

1. Ephesians 6:10-17—The Christian life is a war.

2. Hebrews 12:1—The Christian life is a race.

3. 1 Corinthians 9:26-27—The Christian life is a fight.

4. Titus 3:8—The Christian must be careful to apply himself to good deeds.

5. James 4:7—The Christian must resist the devil (cf. 1 Pet. 5:8).

6. 1 Corinthians 9:27—The Christian must bring his body into subjection.

7. Ephesians 5:15—The Christian must look carefully how he walks.

8. Philippians 3:14—The Christian must "press toward the mark for the prize of the high calling of God in Christ Jesus."

9. 2 Corinthians 7:1—The Christian must "cleanse [himself] from all filthiness of the flesh and spirit, perfecting holiness in the fear of God."

C. The Biblical Balance

It is far too simplistic to say that all that is needed in the Christian life is to let God live it for you. Yet that's what the Quietists emphasized. But they were countered by the Pietists, who were legalists. They said you live the Christian life in the flesh. The right balance is somewhere between the two. We do depend on the strength and power of God, abide in Christ, and count on His divine resources. But there also must be a tremendous level of commitment, self-control, and self-discipline in the Christian life. We must dedicate our lives on a day-to-day basis to fight Satan with all our energy. It is too simple to just surrender.

1. 2 Peter 1:3-7

   a) God's part

   Verse 3 says, "His divine power hath given unto us all things that pertain unto life and godliness, through the knowledge of him that hath called us to glory and virtue." God's divine power equips us to be virtuous. As a Christian, you do not lack any needed resources. Where did you get them? When you came to know God at salvation, He gave you everything you needed.

   Through God's divine power we "are given . . . exceedingly great and precious promises, that by these [we] might be partakers of the divine nature" (v. 4). That is God's part in creating the balance. He makes available the tremendous resource to live the Christian life.

   b) Man's part

   Do we then say, "Now I can surrender and let go and let God?" No. Verses 5-7 say, "Beside this, giving all diligence, add to your faith virtue; and to virtue, knowledge; and to knowledge, self-control; and to self-control, patience; and to patience, godliness; and to godliness, brotherly kindness; and to brotherly kindness, love." In other words, get on with living. Your life is not as simple as walking down an aisle and surrendering. That is part of your life, but you also must be committed to the lordship of Christ and acknowledge His power and resources in your life.

2. Romans 6:12; 8:13

There is certainly a place for yielding ourselves (Rom. 6:13), but there also is a place for killing the deeds of the flesh (Rom. 8:13). The Christian life is not simple. That's why we need to proclaim the truths of Ephesians 6.

3. Philippians 2:12-13

    Verse 12 says, "Wherefore, my beloved, as ye have always obeyed, not as in my presence only but now much more in my absence, work out your own salvation with fear and trembling." The key is a life of obedience. Verse 13 says, "For it is God who worketh in you both to will and to do of his good pleasure." God works out His will in your life and you are to obey Him. That's the balance.

4. Colossians 1:29

    Paul says, "For this I also labor, striving according to his working, which worketh in me mightily." I work and God works. That's why I say it's far too simplistic to elevate the concept of surrender. There must be commitment in my life to self-discipline and obedience. If you take the view that you should just let go and let God, what are you going to do with all the New Testament exhortations? If the Lord does everything, then those exhortations should have been directed at Him, not you. There is a balance between yielding to the lordship of Christ and committing yourself to be disciplined in obedience.

5. 2 Corinthians 6:4-7

    We're to be "in all things commending ourselves as the ministers of God, in much patience, in afflictions, in necessities, in distresses, in stripes, in imprisonments, in tumults, in labors, in watchings, in fastings; by pureness, by knowledge, by long-suffering, by kindness, by the Holy Spirit, by love unfeigned, by the word of truth, by the power of God, by the armor of righteousness on the right hand and on the left." That is a phenomenal blending of our attitudes and actions with the resources of God. What are those resources? The Holy Spirit, divine love, the Word of the truth (the Bible), the power of God, and the armor of righteousness (vv. 6-7). So we depend on God and give our all.

Ephesians 6:13-17 doesn't contradict the Bible; the people who have taught you that all you need to do is surrender have missed the point. There is far more to the Christian life than that. They have taught that the only way to grow in the Christian life is through total surrender, but the Bible teaches that you grow by being obedient with daily commitment to Jesus Christ. You don't grow by no effort; you grow by maximum effort.

Review

We are in a battle. Winning it demands our greatest effort, so we must put on the armor of God.

I. THE BELT OF TRUTHFULNESS (v. 14a; see p. 65)

II. THE BREASTPLATE OF RIGHTEOUSNESS (v. 14b; see p. 79)

III. THE SHOES OF THE GOSPEL OF PEACE (v. 15; see p. 103)

IV. THE SHIELD OF FAITH (v. 16; see p. 117)

V. THE HELMET OF SALVATION (v. 17a; see p. 135)

    A. The Soldier's Helmet (see p. 135)

    B. The Saint's Salvation (see p. 135)

What does the helmet of salvation mean? It doesn't mean becoming saved. You wouldn't be wearing any of the pieces of armor if you weren't saved. You don't get saved fifth; you get saved first. The helmet of salvation refers to something other than the act of saving grace. We are in the army. That assumes we are saved.

       1. The theology of salvation (see p. 136)

Salvation has three dimensions: past, present, and future. The only definition of salvation the Bible gives is a three-dimensional one. The Bible doesn't define salvation as valid only in the past, the present, or in the future. We have been saved, we are being saved, and we will be saved. Our past justification results in sanctification, which promises glorification. We were saved from the penalty of sin in the past, we are saved from the power of sin in the present, and we will be saved from the presence of sin in the future.

       2. The testimony of Scripture (see p. 137)

The dimension that Paul specifically alludes to here is the future. The helmet of salvation is not dealing with the past or present but with the future. The future of your salvation is a protection against the broadsword of Satan.

C. Satan's Sword (see p. 139)

Satan uses a big broadsword that has two edges: discouragement and doubt. Your protection is the helmet of salvation.

1. Discouragement (see p. 140)
   a) A representative illustration (see p. 140)
   b) A relentless battle (see p. 141)
   c) A renewed encouragement (see p. 142)

Lesson

   d) A remembered hope

When you get discouraged, remember a great and glorious day is coming when there will be a celebration of victory. When you become weary, remember that you will reap if you don't faint (Gal. 6:9). Someday there will be a reward for you when Jesus faces you and says, "Well done, good and faithful servant" (Matt. 25:23). Satan will try to hit you with discouragement when you grow weary from fighting the battle. The struggle often seems endless. That is the time to remember that a day of victory is coming. There is a finish line to your race. We will stand face-to-face with Jesus Christ at that glorious moment.

The helmet of salvation offers confidence in the future. In 1 Thessalonians 5:8 Paul calls it "the hope of salvation." The helmet gives us strength to live in the present, even when things get tough. There is a finish line with a glorious reward. The end is in view; the coronation day is coming when we will leave this vale of tears and enter into the presence of Jesus Christ. Our flesh will fall aside and there will be no more sin and struggle. We will live in a glorious new universe. But we can enjoy that future now by having a complete commitment to Christ. Satan wants to discourage you in the battle, but realize that the day of victory is coming—so don't bail out.

If there were no future element to salvation, the other two elements would be meaningless. If I was saved and am being saved, but had no future salvation, why should I fight so hard? If there is no hope of a final element of salvation, why put out all the effort?

   e) A resurrection future

156

(1) 1 Corinthians 15:32—Paul says, "If, after the manner of men, I have fought with beasts as Ephesus, what doth it profit me, if the dead rise not? Let us eat and drink; for tomorrow we die," Paul is saying, "If there's no future in this life, forget it. If I have to go into Ephesus and face persecution so severe that I have to fight with wild beasts, what would it profit me if there's no resurrection? Do you think I'm going to lay my life on the line for a bunch of wild animals? Do you think I'm going to confront hostile pagans with Christ's gospel if there's no resurrection? I would give up right now and throw in the towel!" A salvation with no future would have no power to cause me to fight the battle today.

(2) 2 Corinthians 4:6-11, 14—"For God, who commanded the light to shine out of darkness, hath shone in our hearts, to give the light of the knowledge of the glory of God in the face of Jesus Christ" (v. 6). God has put Christ in our hearts to radiate His light to the world. Verse 7 says, "But we have this treasure [the light of God] in earthen vessels, that the excellency of the power may be of God, and not of us." We have divine power in the indwelling Christ. What are the results? Verses 8-11 say, "We are troubled on every side, yet not distressed; we are perplexed, but not in despair; persecuted, but not forsaken; cast down, but not destroyed; always bearing about in the body the dying of the Lord Jesus. . . . For we who live are always delivered unto death for Jesus' sake." What is it like to minister for Christ? Paul was always living day-to-day on the edge of death while confronting a godless, hostile world. You might ask why he bothered. Verse 14 says, "Knowing that he who raised up the Lord Jesus shall raise up us also by Jesus." Paul's level of commitment was sustained because he knew that someday he would be raised to glory with Christ. The future dimension of salvation should be a powerful force in our lives.

Someday I'm going to stand face-to-face with Jesus Christ, who knows the record of what I've done to serve Him. I love Him enough to give everything I can give. As long as God gives me breath in this life—which is a vapor that appears for a little while and then vanishes away (James 4:14)—I want to maximize those few short years so I can experience the fullness of glorification in eternity with Christ. I don't want to grow weary in doing good because I know I will reap a glorious reward if I don't faint (Gal. 6:9).

Satan tries to discourage me by saying, "Why don't you quit preaching for awhile and rest? Don't give the people so much to study. Just think up a few things and tell a funny story. They'll never know the difference." Sometimes I get distressed by the things I work hard at. Satan will say, "It is very discouraging to be in the ministry. People don't appreciate you. The church isn't doing the things you want it to do. Why don't you give up on it?" But I keep going because I know the coronation day is coming, when we will be like Christ. We should want to maximize all we can for eternity. That's what moved Paul, and that's what ought to move us. Paul said, "I have fought a good fight, I have finished my course, I have kept the faith; henceforth there is laid up for me a crown of righteousness, which the Lord, the righteous judge, shall give at that day; and not to me only, but unto all them also that love his appearing" (2 Tim. 4:7-8). When Satan attacks us with his sword of discouragement, we are to hold fast and be confident that the salvation God promised will come to pass.

2. Doubt

Satan has another edge on his sword: doubt, the ultimate discouragement.

a) The false doctrine of eternal insecurity

(1) Satan's ploy

Do you know that Satan wants you to doubt your salvation? He is good at that. Most people suffer from that at some point in their Christian life. No one of us is totally invulnerable to Satan's temptations along that line. After you have sinned, Satan will say, "You're not a Christian. Why would the Lord ever save you? You'll never make it—you're not good enough. You don't deserve to be saved. How do you know you received Christ as Savior and Lord? Better try again."

There are people who go to certain churches that teach you can lose your salvation. People ask me, "Do you believe in eternal security?" Yes, because that's what the Bible teaches. One thing I don't believe in is eternal insecurity. But there are some people who live in a state of insecurity all their lives. Some people are taught that you can never know if you're saved until you face the Lord. Can you imagine living like that? What a horrible existence! That would not be a fulfillment of 1 John 1:4: "And these things write we unto you, that your joy may be full." You would have to make it say, "These things are written unto you that you might be miserable"! You could never be happy knowing that your salvation was a guessing game.

There are other people who think that every time you sin, you lose your salvation. One man on television was being asked questions. Someone called up and asked, "If you sin as a Christian, but you forget to confess it before the rapture comes, what happens?" He said, "You'll go to hell." Can you imagine living under that kind of fear?

(2) Satan's purpose

Satan wants us to doubt our salvation because he wants us to doubt the promise of God. He wants us to believe that God doesn't keep His Word. He wants us to believe that God can't hold onto us forever. He wants us to deny God's power and resources. He also wants us to deny that God speaks the truth.

b) The true doctrine of eternal security

How do you react to Satan's attack of doubt? The helmet of salvation assures you that if you were saved in the past, you will be saved in the future. There is no other kind of salvation in the Bible but that which involves justification, sanctification, and glorification. Romans 8:30 says, "Whom he called, them he also justified; and whom he justified, them he also glorified."

(1) Security in the Trinity

(*a*) God's gifts to Christ

John 6:37 says, "All that the Father giveth me shall come to me; and him that cometh to me I will in no wise cast out." The phrase "in no wise" means, "under no circumstances." There are no circumstances under which Christ would cast out someone who came to Him. Why? Because the only ones who come are those whom the Father gives. If God gives you to Christ, it is by the decree of God. Then Christ responds to that decree by keeping you. There is no way to lose. The Father rewards the Son with gifts for going to the cross and accomplishing redemption. Those lovely gifts are the souls of men. You and I who know Christ are gifts from the Father to the Son—tokens of the Father's love. The Father loves the Son so much that He gives those kinds of gifts. Conversely, the Son loves the Father so much that He holds tightly to such precious gifts. Under no circumstances would He turn them away. Why? Because the Son loves the Father too much to ever lose anyone who was a love gift from the Father.

(*b*) God's will for Christ

John 6:38 says, "For I came down from heaven, not to do mine own will but the will of him that sent me." That was the Father's plan: to redeem some people, give them to the Son, and have the Son keep them. Verse 39 says, "And this is the Father's will who hath sent me, that of all that he hath given me I should lose nothing, but should raise it up again at the last day." How many does Jesus lose? None. There is no loss between the decree of the Father, the gift to the Son, and the resurrection on the last day. The Bible teaches that God has a counsel that cannot be changed, a calling that cannot be revoked, an inheritance that cannot be defiled, a foundation that cannot be shaken, and a seal that cannot be broken.

(2) Strands in the rope of security

John 10:27-29 describes seven strands in the rope that binds us eternally to Christ.

(a) The character of the Shepherd

Verse 27 says, "My sheep." Whose sheep are you? Christ's. If you are Christ's sheep, it is His duty as a Shepherd to care for you and protect you. If He loses you that is a slur against His own ability as a Shepherd. If you are His sheep, and the Shepherd is to care for the sheep, then if someone is lost, it reflects upon the character and quality of the Shepherd.

(b) The character of the sheep

Verse 27 says, "My sheep hear my voice, and I know them, and they follow me." Christ's sheep follow Him with no exceptions. They will not listen to strangers; they will listen only to Him. True Christians are kept by the power of the great Shepherd and will follow Him. They may stumble and sin, but they will still be with Him.

(c) The definition of eternal life

Verse 28 says, "And I give unto them eternal life." How long does eternal life last? Forever. To speak of it as ending is a contradiction in terms. So we are bound by the very definition of eternal life.

(d) The definition of a gift

Verse 28 says, "I give unto them." You didn't do anything to earn eternal life, and you can't do anything to keep it. It is a gift.

(e) The truthfulness of Christ

Verse 28 also says, "They shall never perish." If one Christian ever did, then Christ didn't tell the truth. If Christ didn't tell the truth,

161

then throw away your Bible and forget Christianity. It would have to be wrong.

(f) The power of Christ

Verse 28 then says, "Neither shall any man pluck them out of my hand."

(g) The power of the Father

Verse 29 says, "My Father, who gave them to me, is greater than all, and no man is able to pluck them out of my Father's hand." Notice that in verse 28 Christ says, "My hand," and in verse 29, "My Father's hand." That's double protection.

In His own words Jesus confirms that a past salvation includes a future one. Eternal life is just that; we never perish. Christ will never lose any of us. No wonder the apostle Paul says, "For I am persuaded that neither death, nor life, nor angels, nor principalities, nor powers, nor things present, nor things to come, nor height, nor depth, nor any other creation, shall be able to separate us from the love of God, which is in Christ Jesus, our Lord" (Rom. 8:38-39). Paul is saying there is nothing in the universe now or in the future that could ever separate a believer from Christ. Philippians 1:6 says to be "confident of this very thing, that he who hath begun a good work [past aspect of salvation] in you will perform it [present aspect] until the day [future aspect] of Jesus Christ." All three elements of salvation are in the same verse.

(3) Survival in the days of apostasy

I want to close our study by looking at the book of Jude.

(a) A description of apostates

Jude was written to deal with apostasy, which is a departure from the faith. It primarily describes the vile character of false prophets and teachers. Verse 4 says, "For there are certain men crept in unawares, who were before of old ordained to this condemnation, ungodly men, turning the grace of our God into lasciviousness." Jude describes them as filthy dreamers (v. 8); prophets who prophesied for greed (v. 11); clouds without water, trees without fruit, twice dead, plucked up by the roots (v. 12); raging waves of the sea, and wandering stars, to whom is reserved the blackness of darkness forever (v. 13). Verse 16 says apostates "are murmurers, complainers, walking after their own lusts."

(b) A description of the remnant

There was a small group of Christians in the midst of the apostasy that Jude described—not unlike us today. Right in the midst of vile, evil, false teaching and the corruption of the church was a group of believers who might have thought they would get swept up in all the apostasy. They saw all the values of society going down the drain. In our society liberalism and neo-orthodoxy seem to be taking over Christianity. We wonder if we're going to fall to that influence. In verses 1 and 24-25, Jude says that we don't have to fear, no matter how vile the world around us becomes.

i) Jude 1—"Jude, the servant of Jesus Christ, and brother of James, to them that are sanctified by God, the Father, and [kept by] Jesus Christ." In the midst of all the rot around them, they were set apart by God and kept by Jesus Christ. The Greek verb *tēreō* means "to watch," "to guard," "to keep," or "to preserve." It has been used outside the Bible to refer to something being guaranteed. When you were saved, you were given a guarantee. The Bible says that we've been given the Spirit as "the earnest of our inheritance" (Eph. 1:14). That refers to a down payment or guarantee. When you were saved, God gave you the Holy Spirit as a guarantee that someday you would be glorified in the presence of God.

Jesus prayed that the Father would keep

the believer from the evil one (John 17:15). Jesus' prayer will be answered. You are not only sanctified, but also kept by Jesus Christ. That's the purpose of the helmet of salvation. You don't need to listen to Satan's doubts, but you better make sure you're a Christian. If you're not confident of that, you can't have any confidence at all. If you don't have any confidence, you are either not a Christian, or you are a Christian who is being attacked by Satan. You had better put on the helmet of salvation!

ii) Jude 24-25—"Now unto him that is able to keep you from falling" (v. 24). The word translated "able" is *dunamai* in the Greek text. It means "power." Christ is powerful enough to prevent you from falling. Verse 24 continues. "And to present you faultless [Gk., *amōmos*]." *Amōmos* is used in 1 Peter 1:19 to refer to Christ. Christ is able to keep you from stumbling and to present you to God as pure as Christ is pure. That is the keeping power of Christ. That is tremendous security.

The Greek word for "keep" in verse 24 is not *tēreō*, but is *phulassō*, which means, "to secure in the midst of an attack." No matter what the hosts of hell throw against you, Christ is powerful enough to keep you from falling and to present you as spotless as He Himself is in the presence of God.

The psalmist said, "Surely goodness and mercy shall follow me all the days of my life; and I will dwell in the house of the Lord forever" (Ps. 23:6). He knew that the salvation God gave him was past, present, and future.

In 1 Thessalonians 5:23-24 Paul offers this glorious benediction: "The very God of peace sanctify you wholly; and I pray God your whole spirit and soul and body be preserved blameless unto the coming of our Lord Jesus Christ. Faithful is he that calleth you, who also will do it." We do not accept the blows of doubt that Satan casts against us. Our armor gives us confidence that salvation is future, as well as present and past. Christ holds us in the power of His own hand. Hebrews 6:15-19 says there are two immutable things: the promise of Christ and the oath of Christ. Our hope in those things is the anchor of the believer's soul. That confidence enables us to defend ourselves against Satan's blows.

When Satan comes with discouragement and doubt, be assured that the day of glory is coming. Fight the good fight. Have confidence in the salvation God gave you.

In the wonderful hymn "The Church's One Foundation," nineteenth-century lyricist Samuel J. Stone said,

> 'Mid toil and tribulation,
> And tumult of her war,
> She waits the consummation
> Of peace forevermore;
> Till with the vision glorious
> Her longing eyes are blest,
> And the great Church victorious
> Shall be the Church at rest.

Someday there will be that rest. Right now we're in the battle. The rest comes when the victory is ours. George Duffield, in the hymn "Stand Up, Stand Up for Jesus," said,

> Stand up, stand up for Jesus,
> The strife will not be long;
> This day the noise of battle,
> The next, the victor's song;
> To him that overcometh
> A crown of life shall be;
> He with the King of glory
> Shall reign eternally.

Don't give up. Don't let Satan victimize you with discouragement, and don't doubt because you are going to win in the end. Keep your helmet on!

Focusing on the Facts

1. What group has become a main advocate of the theory of surrendering (see p. 150)?
2. Explain the concept of surrendering to the Lord as supported by Charles Trumbull and Hannah Whitall Smith (see pp. 151-52).

3. List some verses that counteract the teaching of surrendering. How do they characterize the Christian life (see p. 152)?

4. Explain the balance we must have in living the Christian life (see p. 153).

5. According to 2 Peter 1:3-7, what is God's part in helping you to live the Christian life? What is your part (see p. 153)?

6. According to 2 Corinthians 6:6-7, what are our resources from God (see p. 154)?

7. What is an important thing to remember about your future whenever you get discouraged (see p. 156)?

8. Why would an absence of a future element to salvation render the first two elements meaningless (see p. 156)?

9. According to 2 Corinthians 4:8-11, what is it like to minister for Jesus Christ? According to verse 14, what was Paul's motivation for ministering (see p. 157)?

10. According to 2 Timothy 4:7-8, what motivated Paul throughout his life (see p. 158)?

11. How does Satan use doubt to cause problems in a believer's life? Why does he want us to doubt (see pp. 158-59)?

12. How does the helmet of salvation protect the believer from Satan's attack of doubt (see p. 160)?

13. Why would Christ never lose any believer who has come to Him (John 6:37; see p. 160)?

14. According to John 6:39, what is God's will for Christ (see p. 160)?

15. What are the seven strands in the rope that binds the believer to Christ? Explain each one (John 10:27-29; see pp. 161-62).

16. Find each of the three elements of salvation in Philippians 1:6 (see p. 162).

17. How does Jude describe apostates (see p. 162)?

18. How did Jude encourage the Christian remnant in Jude 1 (see p. 163)?

19. In what condition does Christ present you to God (Jude 24; see p. 164)?

Pondering the Principles

1. Read 2 Peter 1:3-11. According to verses 3-4, what has God given to those whom He has saved? According to verses 5-7, what do we have to add to our faith? According to verse 9, what will happen to you if you are not diligently adding to your faith the things of verses 5-7? What do you have to start doing to provide the appropriate balance in your life between what God has done for you and what you need to do?

2. Read 2 Corinthians 4:8-14 and 2 Timothy 4:6-7. What motivated

Paul to endure the things he did? What motivates you to do all you can in this life? Are you maximizing your time? Based on your answers, do you think Christ is pleased with your level of commitment? What do you think you need to do to be ready for the day you appear before Christ and give account for what you have done?

3. Examine the seven strands of the rope that binds you to Christ (see pp. 161-62). Record any weak strands that you need to strengthen. Do you view Christ as your Shepherd who protects you from all the attacks of the devil? Do you listen to Christ's voice only, avoiding the voices of those propagating strange doctrines? Do you remember that your life as a believer is eternal? Do you remember that your salvation was a gift from God and that you did nothing to deserve it? Do you trust Christ in all things, knowing that He will never lie? Do you trust both God and Christ for their power to keep you saved? If you are weak in any of those areas, begin to strengthen those strands today.

10
The Believer's Armor—
Part 7

Outline

Introduction
A. The Authorship of the Bible
B. The Inspiration of the Bible
C. The Resources of the Bible

Review
  I. The Belt of Truthfulness
 II. The Breastplate of Righteousness
III. The Shoes of the Gospel of Peace
IV. The Shield of Faith
 V. The Helmet of Salvation

Lesson
VI. The Sword of the Spirit
    A. The Roman's Sword
    B. The Christian's Sword
       1. Its translation
          a) A sword that is spiritual
          b) A sword that is given by the Spirit
       2. Its teacher
       3. Its effectiveness
       4. Its power
          a) In salvation
          b) In judgment
       5. Its capabilities
          a) Defensive
              (1) Learning from Christ's pattern
              (2) Learning the specific principles
          b) Offensive
              (1) An illustrative parable
                  (a) The sower's fruit

(b)   The devil's attack
      i)   Through demons
      ii)   Through persecution
      iii) Through deceit
(2)   An important principle
    (a)   Identified
    (b)   Illustrated

Introduction

The last piece of the Christian's armor is in Ephesians 6:17. Paul expresses what is needed for the believer to overcome Satan and his hosts when he says to take "the sword of the Spirit, which is the word of God." One old saint said that the Bible is "an armory of heavenly weapons, a laboratory of infallible medicines, a mine of exhaustless wealth. It is a guidebook for every road, a chart for every sea, a medicine for every malady, a balm for every wound. Rob us of our Bible, and our sky has lost its sun."

A.   The Authorship of the Bible

One writer said this: "The authorship of this book is wonderful. Here are words written by kings, by emperors, by princes, by poets, by sages, by philosophers, by fishermen, by statesmen, by men learned in the wisdom of Egypt, educated in the schools of Babylon, trained at the feet of rabbis in Jerusalem.

"It was written by men in exile, in the desert, in shepherds' tents, in green pastures and beside still waters.

"Among its authors we find a taxgatherer, a herdsman, a gatherer of sycamore fruits; we find poor men, rich men, statesmen, preachers, captains, legislators, judges, exiles.

"The Bible is a library filled with history, genealogy, ethnology, law, ethics, prophecy, poetry, eloquence, medicine, sanitary science, political economy, and the perfect rules for personal and social life." Behind every word is the divine author: God Himself.

John Wesley said that the Bible could have only been written by God, good men, bad men, angels, or devils. Bad men or devils would not write it because of the condemnation of sin and pronouncement of fearful judgment upon the sinner. Good men or angels would not deceive men by lying about its authority and claiming that God was the writer. Therefore the

Bible must have been written as it claims to have been written, by God who by His Spirit inspired men to record His words, using the human instrument to communicate its truth.

I'm quite confident that we don't understand the fullness of what it means to have the sword of the Spirit. This incredible, matchless, incomparable book is the final weapon—the final element of armor given to the believer in the battle against Satan. But sadly, many Christians do not know how to use it. We fall victim to Satan because of an inept use of the sword.

B. The Inspiration of the Bible

Do you realize what kind of a book the Bible is? Let me show you what the Bible claims:

1. It is infallible

The Bible is without error in total. The sum of its parts makes no mistakes. It is faultless, flawless, and without blemish. Psalm 19:7 says, "The law of the Lord is perfect."

2. It is inerrant

There are no errors in its parts. Proverbs 30:5-6 says, "Every word of God is pure. . . . Add thou not unto his words, lest he reprove thee, and thou be found a liar." God's Word is infallible in total and inerrant in its parts.

3. It is complete

Revelation 22:18-19 says, "If any man shall add unto these things, God shall add unto him the plagues that are written in this book; and if any man shall take away from the words of the book of this prophecy, God shall take away his part from the tree of life." You can't add to the Bible or take away from it; it is complete.

4. It is authoritative

Isaiah 1:2 says, "Hear, O heavens, and give ear, O earth; for the Lord hath spoken." When God speaks, everyone had better listen!

5. It is sufficient

Second Timothy 3:15 says Scripture is sufficient to make you "wise unto salvation." It is sufficient to make you "perfect, thoroughly furnished unto all good works" (v. 17). This book can bring you to salvation and perfection.

6. It is effective

When the Bible speaks, things happen. The Word of God changes things—it works a transformation. Isaiah 55:11 says, "So shall my word be that goeth forth out of my mouth; it shall not return unto me void, but it shall accomplish that which I please." If I didn't believe that, I wouldn't preach it. I preach the Bible because I believe it will do what it says it will do.

7. It is divine

Second Peter 1:20-21 says, "No prophecy of the scripture is of any private interpretation. For [Scripture] came not at any time by the will of man, but holy men of God spoke as they were infallible, inerrant, complete, authoritative, sufficient, effective, and divine ought to be cherished.

8. It is determinative

What a person does with the Bible reveals his relationship to God. In John 8:47 Jesus says, "He that is of God heareth God's words; ye, therefore, hear them not, because ye are not of God." If you follow the teachings of the Bible, that shows you belong to God. If you don't listen to it, that shows you don't belong to Him. In that sense, the Bible becomes a determiner of a man's eternal destiny and his relationship with God.

What an incredible book! There is no book in existence that can make those claims and substantiate them.

C. The Resources of the Bible

What resources does the Bible offer you? Let me suggest a few:

1. The source of truth

If there is anything that people in our society are looking for, it is truth. Most people are as cynical as Pilate was when he said, "What is truth?" (John 18:38). He gave up. People are looking for truth. John 17:17 says, "Thy word is truth." It is the truth about life and death, time and eternity, heaven and hell, right and wrong, men and women, old people and young people. It is the truth about children. It is the truth about society. It is the truth about every relationship between God and man, between man and man, and between man and creation. It is the truth about everything that's needful.

2. The source of happiness

The world around us furiously chases after happiness. The simplicity of Scripture is this: "Blessed [happy] is the man who heareth me" (Prov. 8:34). In Luke 11:28 Jesus said, "Blessed [happy] are they that hear the word of God, and keep [obey] it." That is true happiness. The Bible is the source of happiness as well as the source of truth because no man is happier than when he discovers truth.

3. The source of growth

    One night, I watched an interview on television with a lady who had been raped. The interviewer asked her, "What have you learned through this?" She said, "I've grown through this." And the interviewer said, "Growing is what life is all about." Life is all about growing but not in the way they may have thought. The Christian life is about growing in the knowledge of the Word of God. Peter says, "Grow in grace, and in the knowledge of our Lord and Savior, Jesus Christ" (2 Peter 3:18). How do you do that? First Peter 2:2 says, "As newborn babes, desire the pure milk of the word, that ye may grow by it."

4. The source of power

    We are impotent if we don't use God's Word because the Bible is the source of our power. Hebrews 4:12 says, "For the word of God is living, and powerful, and sharper than any two-edged sword."

5. The source of guidance

    Psalm 119:105 says, "Thy word is a lamp unto my feet, and a light unto my path."

6. The source of comfort

    Romans 15:4 says that the Scripture gives us comfort.

7. The source of perfection

    Second Timothy 3:17 says Scripture is given "that the man of God may be perfect." The Bible has no errors. It is always sufficient and complete. It is authoritative, effective, and determinative. It can bring truth, happiness, growth, power, guidance, comfort, and perfection to your life.

8. The source of victory

    That brings us to Ephesians 6:17: "The sword of the Spirit, which is the word of God," is our weapon against the enemy.

I systematically teach the Word of God because the truth of the Bible can't help you if you never learn it. You would never use your resource. The Word of God is the source of truth, happiness, growth, power, guidance, comfort, perfection, and victory.

Review

Ephesians 6:10-12 has made it clear to us that we're in a war. We are wrestling against Satan and his demons. But as Christians, we've been given resources in Christ. We are blessed with all spiritual blessings in the heavenlies (Eph. 1:3). Our resources give us the knowledge of how we are to live. Now we are facing the reality that Satan resists our application of those resources. Satan tries to stop our productivity—to stop us from living out our position in Christ. The only way to overcome his resistance is to have on the armor of God.

I. THE BELT OF TRUTHFULNESS (v. 14a; see p. 65)

II. THE BREASTPLATE OF RIGHTEOUSNESS (v. 14b; see p. 79)

III. THE SHOES OF THE GOSPEL OF PEACE (v. 15; see p. 103)

IV. THE SHIELD OF FAITH (v. 16; see p. 117)

V. THE HELMET OF SALVATION (v. 17a; see p. 155)

Lesson

VI. THE SWORD OF THE SPIRIT (v. 17b)

The previous pieces of armor have been primarily defensive, but now we come to a piece of armor that is both defensive and offensive.

A. The Roman's Sword

The word translated "sword" in Ephesians 6:17 is *machaira* in the Greek text. It is a common word in the Greek language and in the New Testament. The other Greek word for sword is *rhomphaia*, which refers to a large broadsword that could be as long as forty inches. It was a two-edged sword that was wielded with two hands. But that sword is not in view by Paul in verse 17. He is referring to the normal sword carried by the soldier. Its length was anywhere from six to eighteen inches. It was carried in a sheath or scabbard at the soldier's side and was used in hand-to-hand combat.

1. The word *machaira* was used to describe the swords carried by the Roman soldiers who came to capture Jesus while He was in the Garden of Gethsamane (Matt. 26:47).

2. It is the same word used to describe the sword that Peter used to cut off the ear of the servant of the high priest (Matt. 26:51).

3. It is the same word used to describe the sword used to kill James, the brother of John (Acts 12:2).

4. It is the same word used to describe the sword used against the heroes of the faith (Heb. 11:37).

The *machaira* was the routine sword used by soldiers. But it seems apparent that it had to be used in a precise way to be effective. Peter simply cut off an ear with it. I'm sure that if he had used a *rhomphaia*, he would have cut off more than the servant's ear. But the *machaira* had to be used as a precise weapon. And it is that sword that Paul has in mind.

B. The Christian's Sword

1. Its translation

In Ephesians 6:17 Paul says the sword is "of the Spirit." That is *tou pneumatos* in the Greek text. It could be translated, "by the Spirit" or "spiritual." Those are the two best translations.

a) A sword that is spiritual

This translation does not refer to the Holy Spirit, as such. The sword is spiritual in the sense that the weapons of our warfare are not carnal but spiritual (2 Cor. 10:4). Ephesians 6:12 says we are fighting spiritual wickedness.

All the pieces of the believer's armor are spiritual. We have a spiritual belt, breastplate, shoes, shield, and helmet. So the sword can be used in a spiritual sense. A form of the Greek word *pneumatos* is used as an adjective in Ephesians 1:3 and 5:19, so that is a fair way to translate *tou pneumatos* in the context of the book.

b) A sword that is given by the Spirit

175

Perhaps the translation that is more consistent with the rest of the armor is to call *tou pneumatos* a genitive of origin. That refers to where it comes from: the sword given by the Spirit. It is the sword of the Spirit in the sense that the Spirit has given it. A form of *pneumatos* is used in that sense in Ephesians 3:5, so this translation also fits the context.

Putting the two thoughts together gives the idea that our sword is spiritual because it was given to us by the Holy Spirit.

2. Its teacher

When you became a Christian you received the sword in the form of the Bible. An unbeliever may have the Bible, but he does not have in him the resident truth teacher, the Holy Spirit, who makes the Bible meaningful. That's why the natural man doesn't understand the things of God (1 Cor. 2:14). That's why 1 John 2:20 says, "But ye have an unction [anointing] from the Holy One, and ye know all things." Jesus said, "The Comforter, who is the Holy Spirit, whom the Father will send in my name, he shall teach you all things, and bring all things to your remembrance, whatever I have said unto you" (John 14:26). The Spirit of God living in the believer makes the Word of God available. When you become a believer, you receive the Word of God and the Spirit of God. So the sword is available to believers.

3. Its effectiveness

We need to learn how to use the sword. All Christians possess it. We have God's Word and the resident Spirit of God, who makes God's Word a spiritual sword. The Bible is a weapon. The only question is: Do you know how to use it? That depends on how diligently you study the Word of God. The apostle Paul spent three years in Ephesus and said, "I have not shunned to declare unto you all the counsel of God" (Acts 20:27). Why? He wanted to teach them how to use the sword. He wanted them to be able to use it effectively.

4. Its power

Our sword is spiritual. It was not forged in human anvils or tempered in earthly fires; it has a divine origin. It is a powerful and effective weapon. It is so powerful that nothing can overpower it. Any earthly sword pales in light of the invincibility of the Word of God in the hand of a knowledgeable, righteous saint.

a) In salvation

The sword is so powerful that in Romans 1:16 Paul says, "I am not ashamed of the gospel of Christ; for it is the power of God unto salvation." When you wield your sword, people will be saved. You use the sword to tear away souls from the kingdom of darkness. You can cut a swath through Satan's dominion.

b) In judgment

Hebrews 4:12 says, "The word of God is living, and powerful, and sharper than any two-edged sword, piercing even to the dividing asunder of soul and spirit, and of the joints and marrow, and is a discerner of the thoughts and intents of the heart." The word translated "discerner" comes from the Greek word *krinō*, which means "to judge by sifting out the evidence." The Word of God judges people. When you preach the Word, the judgment of God is brought to bear on their lives. It sifts through and weighs their lives in the balance of the Word of God, showing them the reality of their sinfulness. That's why Hebrews 4:13 says, "Neither is there any creature that is not manifest in his sight, but all things are naked and opened unto the eyes of him with whom we have to do."

God's Word wrests souls from the kingdom of darkness. It pierces into the hearts of men, splitting them open, sifting the evidence, and showing them their own sin and guilt before a holy God. It is a powerful weapon. It is so powerful that it can bring truth to error, happiness to sadness, and light to darkness. It can change stagnation into growth. It can make an infantile person mature. The Bible we hold in our hands is a powerful weapon. It is the sword of the Spirit.

5. Its capabilities

The sword is both defensive and offensive.

a) Defensive

A sword is used just as much to parry a blow as it is to inflict one. A defensive use of the Word of God is critical. Satan attacks you with temptations. But you can parry his blows with a proper use of the Word of God.

(1) Learning from Christ's pattern

For example, our Lord was attacked by Satan with three direct temptations (Matt. 4:1-11; Luke 4:1-13). The first one was, "Don't trust God. Make stones into bread. Don't wait for God to supply your needs" (Matt. 4:3). But Jesus responded with a quote from Deuteronomy 8:3 that was related exactly to that temptation (v. 4). Then Satan said, "Dive off the Temple and let God catch you" (v. 6). Satan wanted Christ to trust God for a wrong desire. But Jesus used Deuteronomy 6:16 to deal with that temptation (v. 7). Then Satan said, "Bow down to me" (v. 9). Once more Jesus used Scripture, Deuteronomy 6:13, to deal exactly with that temptation. Christ precisely used the sword of the Word. He didn't flail it around indiscriminately.

(2) Learning the specific principles

You have to be able to defend yourself from whatever angle temptation comes. There are Christians who own Bibles—who have sat in churches and Bible classes—but don't know the principles for stopping the attack. I have discovered that Satan will find an area where you don't know the biblical principles and that's where he'll start his attack. I've heard this many times: "I didn't know the Bible taught that or I never would have done it." People get themselves into situations that could have been avoided had they known the truth. Use the Bible as a defensive weapon. Learn how to apply the specifics of the Word of God to the specifics of temptation.

Ephesians 6:17 says, "The sword of the Spirit, which is the Word of God." The Greek word for "word" is not *logos*, which means, "a broad or general reference"; it is *rhēma*, which means "a specific statement." So Paul isn't talking about basic knowledge; he is talking about a specific statement. The sword of the Spirit is the specific statement of God. If you don't know what God specifically says about a particular temptation,

178

you can't deal with it. That's why you must learn to know the Word of God in total so you can know the specifics. When I teach the Bible, I don't just read Scripture, tell three stories, and send everyone away. I try to teach the principle in the text. The principle is the specific statement that God wants you to understand so that you can put it in your reservoir of knowledge to use against Satan.

You must learn the principles of the Word of God. You must "study to show thyself approved unto God" (2 Tim. 2:15). Revelation 12:11 refers to saints who "overcame him [Satan] by the blood of the Lamb, and by the word of their testimony." You will overcome Satan when you know the Word. To defend ourselves, we are dependent on our knowledge of the Word of God. The reason so many Christians fall to temptation is they just don't know how God's Word deals with things. They aren't equipped to use the sword properly.

b) Offensive

I use the Word of God to defend myself against Satan's attacks. Whenever Satan hits me with discouragement, I think of verses that relate to that. A man asked me, "What Bible verses do you use when you get sorrowful? What Bible verses do you use when you want to renew your commitment?" He was asking the right questions. Do you know where to go to defend yourself against sorrow, discouragement, and a lack of commitment? Do you know how to defend yourself against the temptation of the lust of the eyes, the lust of the flesh, and the pride of life? You need to know those things to use the Word defensively, but what about offensively?

I'm glad the Word is both offensive and defensive because I would hate to live on the defensive all the time. I like to be offensive; that's why I love to preach. When I'm preaching, I don't have time for any temptations; I'm trying to whack away some of the jungle in Satan's kingdom with my sword. That's exciting! Every time I take the gospel to an unsaved soul, I see myself whacking through Satan's dominion. Every time someone is redeemed, I see a swath cut through his dark kingdom. When you proclaim the Word of God by teaching it to your children, talking about it to your friends, sharing it with other students, or preaching it from a pulpit, you are cutting your way through Satan's kingdom. I love to be interviewed by someone who is confused about something in our society. I can tell him, "God says this," and attack the system with the sword of the Spirit. I love to stand against the opposition and say what God has to say.

(1) An illustrative parable

Satan knows the Word is effective, so he tries to stop it. He will do anything to silence those who preach the Word. He will do anything to try to undo what they do. In Matthew 13:1-9 Jesus tells the parable of the sower and the seed: "The same day went Jesus out of the house, and sat by the seaside. And great multitudes were gathered together unto him, so that he went into a boat, and sat; and the whole multitude stood on the shore. And he spoke many things unto them in parables, saying, Behold, a sower went forth to sow; and when he sowed, some of the seeds fell by the wayside, and the fowls came and devoured them. Some fell upon stony places, where they had not much earth; and forthwith they sprang up, because they had no deepness of earth. And when the sun was up, they were scorched; and because they had no root, they withered away. And some fell among thorns; and the thorns sprang up, and choked them. But other seeds fell into good ground, and brought forth fruit, some an hundredfold, some sixtyfold, some thirtyfold. Who hath ears to hear, let him hear."

In verses 18-23 Jesus explains what the parable means.

(a) The sower's fruit

The sower is the preacher, or anyone who proclaims the Word of God. The seed is the Word of God. When you sow seed, you are using your sword. What is the result? Verse 8 says that when the seed finds good ground, it will bear fruit.

(b) The devil's attack

Satan knows it can do that, so he is busy trying to make sure it doesn't.

i) Through demons

When the seed falls on the wayside, immediately the fowls come and devour it (v. 4). That refers to Satan's demonic hosts. Somehow they are able to snatch the Word away so that the person has forgotten what he has heard. Perhaps you have talked to someone about the Word, but they go away and forget about it. Satan snatches it out of their mind.

ii) Through persecution

Some of the seed falls on stony places (v. 5). What happens? It springs up for a little while, but there is not much earth. As soon as the sun comes up, it burns the plant because it has no root, and it withers away (v. 6). In verse 21 our Lord says that refers to persecution. Someone might say, "Christianity is interesting. I'm hearing what you are saying about the truth of the Bible." But Satan will bring trouble into his life and he will say, "God, You're not so good after all." He will walk away from the truth under the pressure of persecution or tribulation.

iii) Through deceit

Some of the seed falls among thorns that spring up and choke it (v. 7). Our Lord says that refers to people who seem to believe for a little while but are not willing to say no to the evil system. They want the world, so they walk away from the Word.

Satan is busy twisting people's perspective of the world, bringing heat to bear on their life, or snatching the Word away so they won't remember it. He wants to stop the sowing of the seed. Why? Because he knows if it finds good ground, it will produce fruit. If I didn't believe the Word of God would produce, I would quit preaching and do something else. But it is fantastic to know that when you send it out, the Word of God will never return void but will always accomplish what it should. The Word is powerful—so powerful that the Bible says it restores the soul (Ps. 19:7). No word of man can rout the spiritual hosts of wickedness; only the Word of God can. The sword is defensive—we can defend ourselves with it, and it is offensive—we can conquer Satan's dark kingdom with it.

(2) An important principle

(a) Identified

When you use the Word of God offensively, you must use it with precision. Have you ever been questioned and not had answers because you didn't know what the Bible taught about a certain thing? Some people say, "I would witness, but I'm afraid someone will ask me a question and I won't know the answer." If you are going to be effective in communicating, you have to know the Word in season and out of season (2 Tim. 4:2). You need to be "ready always to give an answer to every man that asketh you a reason of the hope that is in you" (1 Pet. 3:15). We need to know the Word of God.

Cult researcher Walter Martin has said the tragedy of Christianity is that a ninety-day wonder from the Jehovah's Witnesses can take apart a Christian in thirty minutes. In many cases that's true. We don't know the Word like we should. We can't defend ourselves or be offensive. But the more you know the Word, the more you will march through Satan's kingdom, because God's

Word has answers that cut right into the core of his lies.

(b) Illustrated

Romans 10:17 says, "Faith cometh by hearing, and hearing by the word of God." That translation is not the way the Greek text renders it. Saving faith doesn't come from being exposed to just any part of the Word of God. You can't read some verse out of the Bible and have faith as a result. The Greek text should be translated, "Faith comes by hearing a specific statement [Gk., *rhēma*] about Christ." Faith doesn't come by general statements; it comes by specific statements about Christ. People can't be saved unless they hear that Jesus Christ died and rose again the third day for their justification.

You must know the specifics in the Word of God to use it offensively and defensively. There's no sense in being victimized. The tragedy of tragedies is for someone to be a Christian a long time and not be able to use the incomparable sword God has graciously given to him. You might say, "I've tried, but I don't understand it." Don't tell me that. God not only gave you the Book, but also planted in your heart the resident truth teacher. He will teach the Word to you if you'll submit to His teachings. No one can plead ignorance. God will enable you to understand as much as you need to understand to win the victory. I understand it, but I work hard at it. Just because you own a Bible doesn't mean you have a sword; you can own a Bible warehouse and not have a sword if you don't know how to use your Bible defensively and offensively. Jesus gave us the pattern in Luke 10:26 when He asked, "What is written in the [Scriptures]?" That's how you need to approach your life and ministry.

Taking a Stand on Scripture

Commentator D. Martyn Lloyd-Jones gives the following example of using the sword of the Spirit: "[Reformer Martin] Luther was held in darkness by the devil, though he was a monk. He was trying to save himself by works. He was fasting, and sweating, and praying; and yet he was miserable and unhappy, and in bondage. . . . But he was delivered by the word of Scripture—'The just shall live by faith." . . . He proceeded to do all in terms of expositions of the Scriptures. . . . He maintained that the Church is not above the Scriptures. The standard by which you judge even the Church is the Scriptures. And though he was but one man, at first standing alone, he was able to fight . . . twelve centuries of tradition. He did so by taking up 'the sword of the Spirit, which is the Word of God' (*The Christian Soldier: An Exposition of Ephesians 6:10 to 20* [Grand Rapids: Baker, 1978], p. 331). There never would have been the Protestant Reformation if one man hadn't stood up against the erudite errorists and countered their arguments with the Word of God.

The author continues: "Our Protestant Fathers in this country did precisely the same thing. . . . That is why the early Protestants were so concerned that there should be a dependable English translation of the Bible. . . . It was Tyndale's resolve that every ploughman, every boy at the plough, should be able to read and to understand it in order that they might be safeguarded against . . . false teaching" (p. 332). We can thank God for those people. It is essential that the Word of God be known if we are to win the battle.

Are You a Butterfly, a Botanist, or a Bee?

One master of illustrations described three things he saw in a garden among the plants and flowers. The first was a butterfly that alighted on an attractive flower, sat for a second or two, then moved on to another, seeing and touching many lovely blossoms but deriving no benefit from them. Next came a botanist with a large notebook and microscope. He spent some time over each flower and plant and made copious notes of each. But when he had finished, his knowledge was shut away in the notebook; very little of it remained in his mind. Then a busy bee came along, entering a flower here and there and spending some time in each, but emerging from each blossom laden with pollen. It went in empty and came out full.

There are those who read the Bible going from one favorite passage to another but getting little from their reading. Others really study and make notes but do not apply the teachings of Scripture. Others—like the bee—spend time over the Word, reading, marking, and inwardly digesting it. Their minds are filled with wisdom and their lives with heavenly sweetness.

Which one are you? A butterfly, flitting from class to class, Bible study to Bible study, seminar to seminar, and book to book, flapping your pretty wings but never changing? Or are you a botanist—with enough notebooks to sink a small battleship? Or are you a bee coming in empty and going out full, turning your knowledge into the honey that makes life sweet? The sword is available. Are you using it as a weapon to win the victory that's already yours in Jesus Christ?

Focusing on the Facts

1. Who wrote the Bible (see p. 170)?
2. What claims does the Bible make for itself? Explain each one (see pp. 171-72).
3. What resources does the Bible offer to Christians? Explain each one (see pp. 172-73).
4. What truth does the Bible talk about (see p. 172)?
5. What kind of sword was Paul referring to in Ephesians 6:17 (see p. 174)?
6. What are the two possible meanings of "the sword of the Spirit"? Explain each one (see pp. 175-76).
7. What must a person have before the Bible can become a sword to him (John 14:26; see p. 176)?
8. What is learning how to use the sword dependent on (see p. 176)?
9. Give two illustrations of the sword's power (see p. 177).
10. Describe the pattern that Jesus set for the defensive use of the sword against Satan's temptations (Matt. 4:1-11; see p. 178).
11. What does "word" refer to in Ephesians 6:17 (see p. 178)?
12. Why is it important to know the specific statements of God (see p. 179)?
13. What are the three ways that Satan tries to stop the Word of God from bearing fruit? Explain each one (Matt. 13:18-23; see pp. 179-80).
14. When you use God's Word as an offensive weapon, why must you use it with precision (see p. 182)?

15. What specific statements from the Word of God must people know to be saved (Rom. 10:17; see p. 183)?

Pondering the Principles

1. Review the eight claims that the Bible makes for itself (see pp. 171-72). In your own words, write out a definition of each one. Give a verse reference for each one. How would you explain what the Bible is to someone who asked you?
2. Review the eight resources that the Bible offers you (see pp. 172-73). What truths has the Bible taught you? Describe the happiness you have as a Christian. How have you grown since you came to Christ? How has God's Word given you power to live the Christian life? How has the direction of your life changed since you became a Christian? What verses of the Bible give you great comfort? How has the Bible helped you grow toward maturity? What victories over Satan have you experienced? Thank God for His Word and the ministry it has had in your life.
3. Set up a schedule for studying God's Word. Pick a particular book of the Bible or a subject that you want to learn. Set aside a certain amount of time for your study and stick to it. As you study, record all the observations you can from a particular passage. Next, underline key words and phrases and define them in terms of what the passage is saying. Paraphrase each verse of the passage. List the divine truths you have found in the passage. Cross-reference the truths you have found with other passages. Next, evaluate what you have discovered by comparing it with what commentators have said about the passage. Finally, apply what you have learned to your life. If you study God's Word diligently, you will be a skilled swordsman, both offensively and defensively.
4. Examine your commitment to God's Word. Are you a butterfly, a botanist, or a bee (see p. 184)? What should you be? What kind of commitment do you need to make to reflect that? Begin to act on your commitment today.

11
Praying at All Times

Outline

Introduction
A. The Priority of Prayer
B. The Presentation of Our Resources
C. The Problem of Spiritual Atheism
D. The Power of the Armor

Lesson
I. The General Instruction
  A. The Frequency of Prayer
    1. The pattern of prayer
    2. The purpose of prayer
      a) Communication with God
      b) Fellowship with God
    3. The persistence of prayer
      a) Luke 18:1-8
      b) Luke 11:5-10
  B. The Variety of Prayer
  C. The Manner of Prayer
    1. The goal
    2. The guidelines
      a) Pray for specifics
      b) Pray for others
      c) Pray for spiritual issues
        (1) Evaluating the priorities
        (2) Examining Paul's priorities
  D. The Indirect Objects of Prayer
  E. The Qualification for Prayer
    1. The meaning
    2. The method
II. The Specific Illustration
  A. The Intention

B. The Information
  1. Communication
  2. Comfort
C. The Invocation

Introduction

A man named Johann Burchard Freystein, who was born in Germany in 1671, wrote the following words to an old hymn:

Rise my soul, to watch and pray; from thy sleep awaken;
Be not by the evil day unawares o'er taken.
For the foe, well we know, oft his harvest reapeth,
While the Christian sleepeth.

Watch against the devil's snares lest asleep he find thee;
For indeed no pains he spares to deceive and blind thee.
Satan's prey oft are they who secure are sleeping
And no watch are keeping.

But while watching, also pray to the Lord unceasing,
He will free thee, be thy stay, strength, and faith increasing.
O Lord bless in distress, and let nothing swerve me
From the will to serve Thee.

Over one hundred years ago Charlotte Elliot wrote the words for the hymn "Watch and Pray":

"Christian, seek not yet repose,"
Hear thy gracious Saviour say;
Thou art in the midst of foes:
"Watch and pray."

Principalities and powers,
Mustering their unseen array,
Wait for thy unguarded hours:
"Watch and pray."

Watch, as if on that alone
Hung the issue of the day;
Pray, that help may be sent down:
"Watch and pray."

Both of those hymns proclaim that victory over Satan and his hosts involves a tremendous commitment to prayer. That is precisely what the apostle Paul is saying in Ephesians 6:18.

A. The Priority of Prayer

Paul has discussed the warfare of the Christian in Ephesians 6:10-17, focusing on the armor of God in verses 14-17. Now he discusses the theme of prayer. Verse 18 begins, "Praying always." Prayer becomes the closing theme in the letter of Ephesians. It is not mentioned as a part of the Christian's armor because it is more than that. Prayer works in concert with the armor. The apostle Paul is not saying that in addition to the armor, add prayer; he is implying that prayer is woven into the armor. As we make sure we have on the belt of truthfulness, breastplate of righteousness, shoes of the gospel of peace, shield of faith, helmet of salvation, and the sword of the Spirit, we are to be involved in prayer. All through the procedure of arming ourselves and undergoing the demands of the battle, we are to be engaged in prayer. It is the very air we breathe.

I remember reading about cetacean mammals, which are neither fish nor fowl. They can stay in water for a period of time, but at some time they must ascend to the surface and gasp for air. The believer must at all times ascend to the throne of God to breathe the air of prayer. Only then is he be able to exist in the darkness of the world around him. Prayer is like breathing; you don't have to think to breathe because the air exerts pressure on your lungs and forces you to breathe. When a believer doesn't pray, he is holding his breath spiritually. The results are all bad. As you live the Christian life, put on the armor and fight the battle, you have to breathe the air of prayer.

In Bunyan's *The Pilgrim's Progress*, God gave Christian a weapon called "all prayer." He was instructed that when everything else failed, this weapon would enable him to defeat all the fiends that would attack him in the valley of the shadow. But prayer is more than what Bunyan saw it as: It's more than an additional weapon; it is the atmosphere in which all our living and fighting occurs.

That prayer is climactic in the book of Ephesians for a reason; it was planned by God's Holy Spirit. Our Lord urged men to pray always and not to faint (Luke 18:1). He knows that when the battle gets hot, you can faint, grow weary, and abandon the fight if you don't pray. You only have two alternatives: You can either pray or faint—there's no middle ground. So prayer becomes vital in the war. But prayer has more significance than just its context in Ephesians: it also climaxes the letter. Prayer is like the musical crescendo in the great anthem of praise in the book of Ephesians.

B. The Presentation of Our Resources

The book of Ephesians, probably more than any other book in
the entire Bible, presents the resources that are ours in Christ.
It is a catalog of all that is ours as Christians. Peter says we
have "all things that pertain unto life and godliness" (2 Pet.
1:3). Colossians 2:10 says, "Ye are complete in him." Those
statements are magnified to their fullness in the book of
Ephesians. The key is Ephesians 1:3: We are blessed "with all
spiritual blessings in heavenly places in Christ." Paul delineates those blessings for us in all six chapters. Ephesians lifts
us to great heights. It starts us in the heavenlies, and we stay
there for the whole book until we come to Ephesians 6:18. It
is there that God demands we fall on our knees. Prayer
becomes the key to appropriating our resources in Christ. We
cannot float around in glory; we have to come back to the
reality of getting on our knees before God so that the
resources can be implemented in our lives. The book that
begins in the heavenlies ends with us on our knees as Paul
calls us to prayer.

You might think that in a book describing such tremendous
resources, prayer wouldn't be that necessary. What would
we pray for? After all, we are:

1. Super blessed (1:3)
2. Super loved (1:4-6)
3. Forgiven and redeemed (1:7)
4. Abounding in wisdom (1:8)
5. Made spiritually rich (1:11)
6. Secure, having been sealed with the Spirit (1:13)
7. Alive with new life (2:4-6)
8. The objects of eternal grace (2:7)
9. God's masterpiece (2:10)
10. Called to a life of good works that God will perform
    through us (2:10)
11. One with God and with all Christians (2:13-18)
12. Members of God's intimate family (2:19)
13. The habitation of the Holy Spirit (2:22)
14. Powerful beyond our own imagination (3:20)
15. Able to glorify God (3:21)
16. Possessers of the Holy Spirit (4:3)
17. Members of the body of Christ (4:4-6)
18. Recipients of gifts and gifted men that perfect us to do the
    work of the ministry (4:11-13)
19. Recipients of Jesus Christ, who teaches us to walk in new

life (4:20-24)
20. Recipients of the love of God, which enables us to walk in love (5:1-2)
21. Recipients of God's light, which enables us to dwell in light (5:8)
22. Recipients of the wisdom and truth of God, which enables us to walk wisely in the world (5:15-17)
23. Recipients of the power of the fullness of the Spirit of God 5:18)
24. Recipients of the resources that can make every human relationship all that God ever intended it to be (5:21—6:9)
25. Recipients of invincible and powerful armor, against which Satan is helpless, including the sword of the Spirit—the magnificent weapon of the Word of God (6:10-17)

That's a tremendous picture! And it all belongs to a Christian.

C. The Problem of Spiritual Atheism

By the time you have recognized your exalted position in Christ and have seen the resources for effective Christian living, you immediately face a problem. You might call it doctrinal egoism— a problem defined in 1 Corinthians 10:12: "Let him that thinketh he standeth take heed lest he fall." You can become what I would call a spiritual atheist: You believe in God, but you don't need Him. We have great knowledge, information, and resources. We understand our position in Christ. We know what our gifts are. We've seen God's blessing. We've had so much success and so little failure that it is easy for us to forget to acknowledge God. We can fall into the terrible sin of self-dependence and lose our sense of dependence on God. We should pray that God would give us enough success to know He's present and enough failure to need Him desperately. We have so many things going for us in our society and our church, and we have seen such tremendous blessing of God, that it is easy to become smug and reduce everything to gimmicks, programs, and methods. When things in our lives are going smoothly— like our marriage, kids, and church—we can become spiritual atheists who tune God out. The kind of passionate and earnest prayer life that God calls for is not in our hearts.

D. The Power of the Armor

The armor is not mechanical or magical; God needs to infuse the armor and our resources with His power and energy.

There is a latent danger that Christians—who have a knowledge of doctrine, a history of success, and an effective grip on practical spiritual principles—can become satisfied and feel they don't need a passionate and constant prayer life. That's a tragedy. That is why Ephesians begins in the heavenlies and ends with us on our knees. Our resources in Christ depend on prayer. Some of you might have come out of seminary, but when you look at your life you say, "I know so much, but I don't see anything happening." You might be thinking the armor or your resources are either magical or mechanical, but they're not; they're dependent on prayer—the soul of man moving in the presence of God.

Lesson

I. THE GENERAL INSTRUCTION (v. 18)

"Praying *always* with *all* prayer and supplication in the Spirit, and watching thereunto with *all* perseverance and supplication for *all* saints."

There are the four *all's* of prayer. Put each piece of the armor on with prayer. It pervades all that we are and do. It is the all-encompassing element of our lives. It is the air we breathe. There is no time in our lives when we should not be in prayer.

A. The Frequency of Prayer

When are we to pray? Always. Some of you may have come out of backgrounds where you read out of a prayer book or prayed at a certain time. Jewish people pray at certain times. When the early church met for prayer, it was a holdover from Judaism, when certain times of the day were set aside for prayer. But with the New Testament and the birth of the church came a new era. There is to be a constant character to prayer. We are not to pray at set times anymore; we are to pray at all times.

1. The pattern of prayer

   a) Luke 21:36—Jesus indicated that was coming when He said, "Watch ye, therefore, and pray always."

   b) Acts 6:4—The apostles said, "We will give ourselves continually to prayer." The key word is "continually."

   c) Acts 10:2—It was said of Cornelius that he was "a devout man . . . and prayed to God always."

d) Romans 12:12—We are to be "continuing diligently in prayer."

e) Colossians 4:2—"Continue in prayer."

f) Philippians 4:6—"In everything, by prayer."

g) 1 Thessalonians 5:17—"Pray without ceasing."

h) 2 Timothy 1:3—The apostle Paul indicated that he prayed without ceasing. He wrote this to Timothy: "Without ceasing I have remembrance of thee in my prayers night and day."

i) Acts 12:5, 13-16—The church prayed constantly. But even though their prayers were somewhat weak in faith, God answered them.

2. The purpose of prayer

I used to wonder what it means to pray at all times. My life was filled with so many things that there never seemed to be a way I could pray at all times. Obviously you can't carry a little book around and read prayers all day. If you ever visit Israel you will see many Jewish people going through prayers hour after hour in front of the Wailing Wall. Praying "always" has nothing to do with formulas and repetition; it is simply living your life with God-consciousness. Your whole life should rise before God in communion.

a) Communication with God

At one time I wondered how anyone could pray at all times. Now I find very few times when I'm not conscious of God. Everything I see and experience in my life simply becomes a prayer. It is something I share with my Best Friend, something I instantly communicate with God. If I am tempted, immediately I find that the temptation results in a prayer: "Lord, You know what I'm going through. Help me." If I see something good, my first thought is: "God, You're the source of every good and perfect gift. I thank You for that." If I see something evil, I say, "Oh God, make that evil right." If I have an opportunity to meet someone who doesn't know Jesus Christ, my first response is: "Oh God, it's so sad that he doesn't know You. Draw him to Yourself." If I see trouble I say, "God, You're the Deliverer." Life becomes an ascending prayer: All life's thoughts, deeds, and circumstances become a point of communication with God. That's what it means to set your affections on things above (Col. 3:2). That's what it means to think about Christ and be conscious about His presence. Everything becomes a prayer. That's the whole point of the Christian life.

b) Fellowship with God

The reason God saved you was for fellowship. First John 1:3 says, "That which we have seen and heard declare we unto you, that ye also may have fellowship with us; and truly our fellowship is with the Father, and with his Son, Jesus Christ." God wants your fellowship. There is no greater expression of fellowship than prayer. If you've been saved and you don't commune with Him, you're denying Him the purpose for which He redeemed you. That's why we are to pray continually.

3. The persistence of prayer

Colossians 4:2 says, "Continue in prayer." The root word for "continue" in the Greek language is *kartereō*, which means "to be steadfast" or "to be constant." It is used of Moses when Hebrews 11:27 says he endured. In Colossians 4:2 the word has a preposition added to the front that means "to be intense." Paul is indicating that prayer is not an easy and selective communication with the Lord, but a life of persevering and struggling over deep issues. Prayer is a way of life. When your heart is open to God in earnest and persistent prayer, you will be blessed.

Our Lord gives two illustrations in Luke 11 and Luke 18.

a) Luke 18:1-8—Jesus tells a story about an unjust judge. A woman kept coming and begging before him. Finally, the judge did what she wanted. The Lord is saying that if an unjust judge will give something to a persistent lady, what do you think a just God will give to His own child who persists in prayer?

b) Luke 11:5-10—Christ also told the story of a man who bangs on the door of a storeowner to get some food. The owner said, "The store is closed. I'm in bed with my wife and kids. I'm not getting up." But the man kept banging until the owner got up and gave him the bread. Jesus is saying that if a sleepy man who is comfortable in bed will get up and give bread to someone banging on his door, what do you think a loving Father will give to a son who has a need?

The point in both stories is that the woman and the hungry man kept persisting until they got what they wanted. God is saying that if you are persistent and faithful in your prayers, He will hear and answer. Life is to be a constant exercise of prayer. You can know so much about the Christian life and still never think about God. But the purpose of what you have learned is to draw you into the presence of God. The frequency of prayer is always. Everything that comes into your life should provide an opportunity for prayer.

B. The Variety of Prayer

The variety of prayer is "all prayer and supplication." The word translated "prayer" generally means "requests." It is *proseuchē* in the Greek text. The word "supplication" is *deesis* in Greek and means "specific." There are general prayers and specific prayers.

Paul says we are to be praying at all times with all prayer and all supplication. What does he mean by "all prayer and supplication"? All kinds of prayers. There are different ways to pray. Some people think the only way to pray is on your knees. Some think the only way you can pray is with your hands up. Others think you must have your hands folded. Some people think you have to pray out of a prayer book. Paul says, "Pray all the time with all kinds of prayers." If you are going to be praying all the time, you will have to pray in different ways because you will never be in the same position all day. You can pray in public or in private, with loud cries or quiet whispers. It can be deliberate or spontaneous. There can be prayers of request, thanksgiving, confession, and praise. You can be kneeling, standing, lifting up your hands, or lying prostrate. Paul is saying, "Pray all the time in all ways." We're to pray throughout the flow of life.

You can pray at all times, in all circumstances, in whatever situation you're in. After having counted on all the infinite resources that are yours in Christ, don't ever think you're not dependent upon the power of God every moment. Let everything become a prayer. In 1 Timothy 2:8 Paul says, "I will, therefore, that men pray everywhere." If you study the prayers of the Bible, you will find that they were offered in all kinds of positions at all times. Prayer is a way of life. A soldier prays at all times so that whenever the battle starts, he is ready. His life is opened totally to God.

When Is the Best Time to Pray?

At a pastors' conference, one man preached on the subject of morning prayer. He said we are to pray in the morning. He quoted Psalm 63:1: "Early will I seek thee." He looked at passages where men prayed in the morning and used that to support his point. The whole time he was preaching I was looking up Scripture verses that talk about praying in the evening, at noon, and at other times in the day. He had a good point: We are to pray in the morning—but not to the exclusion of any other time. Psalm 55:17 says, "Evening, and morning, and at noon, will I pray." Daniel prayed three times a day (Dan. 6:10). Luke 6:12 says that Jesus "continued all night in prayer to God." First Timothy 5:5 says that godly widows "continueth in supplications and prayers night and day." Prayer is a way of life.

Which Is More Important: Prayer or Knowledge?

In a sense, prayer is more important than knowledge. Commentator D. Martyn Lloyd-Jones said, "Our ultimate position as Christians is tested by the character of our prayer life" (*The Christian Soldier: An Exposition of Ephesians 6:10 to 20* [Grand Rapids: Baker, 1978], p. 342). You may have a great deal of knowledge—you may be a seminary student, seminary graduate, minister, pastor, missionary, or Bible teacher—but your prayer life will be a monitor of how deep your relationship to God is. Why? Theology is the knowledge of God. The more theology I know, the more I know about God. The more I know about God, the more I ought to be driven to follow close behind Him. If I say I have great knowledge, but am not driven to be in God's presence all my waking hours, then it is questionable what effect my knowledge has had on my life. John 17:3 says, "And this is life eternal, that they might know thee, the only true God, and Jesus Christ, whom thou hast sent." That is why I study. I want to learn the Word so I might know God. The more I know Him, the more I want to be in His presence. If you know all that, but don't hunger and thirst to be in His presence and keep the lines of communication open with Him every waking moment, then it is questionable that your theology has had the proper effect.

We are to pray at all times with all kinds of prayers. Our lives are to be open to God. He wants us to know Him because fellowship is His desire. Is your life a constant prayer?

C. The Manner of Prayer

Paul said, "Watching thereunto with all perseverance and supplication" (Eph. 6:18). We are to watch with all perseverance.

1. The goal

The idea of perseverance means "to stick to it" or "to continue." We are to pray continuously while watching. Prayer involves being alert to the issues. Jesus said, "Watch ye and pray" (Mark 14:38). First Peter 4:7 says, "Watch unto prayer." You can't pray properly unless you see what is happening. When your heart is filled with prayer, it will be the result of seeing what is going on around you.

My wife and I have realized that it is harder for us to pray these days because there is so much to pray for. We live in a day of tremendous communication. I get mail from radio listeners, tape listeners, and people in the mission fields. The church has many needs. The prayer sheet that comes out every week boggles my mind. There are so many things going on that sometimes I say, "Lord, I don't even know what to say to You other than read the prayer list." I try to keep a prayer list. If I prayed without ceasing, I still couldn't pray for all the things that are in my heart. But I have to keep watching and be alert to needful things.

2. The guidelines

a) Pray for specifics

I want to pray specifically because when God answers, I give Him glory. John 14:13 says, "And whatever ye shall ask in my name, that will I do, that the Father may be glorified in the Son." God answers prayer to put His power on display. If you don't pray specifically, then He can't display Himself.

My daughter Marcy used to pray like this when she was little: "God bless the whole wide world." I would say, "Marcy, you can't pray that way. He won't make the whole world feel better. That's too general; you need to pray about specifics." Our children have become adapted to that. We pray for specifics and God answers specifically. And we give Him glory.

b) Pray for others

Do you know what is going on in the people around you? The word "watch" indicates that we are to be looking outward rather than inward. We know our own problems, but that's not where we need to spend our prayer time. We need to pray for other people, watching for their needs. But selfishness kills that perspective. Most of us never get serious about prayer until some trouble occurs in our own lives. We are often ten times more intense about our own problems than we are about anyone else's. That reveals our self-centeredness. Do you lose yourself in the needs of others like the apostle Paul did? He said, "I ceased not to warn everyone night and day with tears" (Acts 20:31). Have you ever prayed for anyone night and day with tears? You may have wept a few tears over your own troubles, but I doubt if many of us have wept over someone else's problems. That shows the self-centeredness of the human heart. We are to watch "with all perseverance [Gk., *proskarterēsis*]" (Eph. 6:18). We are to watch intensely and steadfastly, being alert to the needs of others.

c) Pray for spiritual issues

(1) Evaluating the priorities

We also need to get past physical needs. We pray for someone's rheumatism, heart problems, broken leg, and surgery. We need to pray for those things, but they are near the bottom of my prayer list. I'm more concerned about the spiritual battle. Are the believers winning the battle? The physical is immaterial by comparison. What gets my heart anxious is someone who is not seeing victory in their life and seeing God do His mighty work. I am praying for the advancement of the kingdom of God in the lives of His people. I am praying for souls to be won to Jesus Christ. It is hard for me to put physical needs at the top of my list, although I realize they have a tremendous effect on our spiritual lives. Paul is saying that we are in a war and we are to pray constantly about it. It is not easy to fight the battle. I pray for people's physical needs, but more than that I pray that God will give them victory in the battle against the enemy. I don't really care what happens to my physical body as long as I gain victory for the glory of God.

(2) Examining Paul's priorities

When Paul had a prayer request, he didn't say, "Pray for me; I'm in jail. The chain is rubbing my right leg raw." Paul said, "[Pray] for me, that utterance may be given unto me, that I may open my mouth boldly to make known the mystery of the gospel" (Eph. 6:19). In other words, "Pray that when Satan tempts me to shut my mouth, I will win out over the temptation and speak the gospel. Pray that I will win the battle."

We are to be involved in making supplications for each other, persistently watching to see what the needs are. Do you know the needs of the people around you? Do you know the spiritual needs of your spouse, children, friends, neighbors, and people in your Bible study? Do you pray for them as they fight the battle? Sometimes all we ever do is pray when disaster comes. Maybe a little preventative prayer could have helped.

D. The Indirect Objects of Prayer

Paul says we are to pray always "for all saints" (v. 18). We are to pray for each other. It doesn't tell us to pray for ourselves. That isn't the priority. I have a personal commitment in my life not to pray for myself. I realize that I have needs, and I do ask the Lord's help regarding sinful things in my life and I confess those things to Him. But as far as concentrating on myself, I trust what Scripture says and pray for others instead. I know I am covered in prayer, because others pray for me.

It is wonderful when we can give ourselves to pray for others. One man told me, "Your ministry has blessed me so much that I'm going to put you on my prayer list for six months." He made a commitment to pray for me, and I prayed for him because I knew he would be praying for me for those six months. I felt responsible to pray for him. That is the way the body of Christ grows in love. We don't have to wait for our own trouble to pray; we can learn to pray by praying for others. The apostle Paul illustrates that so well because he always prayed for everyone else. First Samuel 12:23 says, "God forbid that I should sin against the Lord in ceasing to pray for you." Don't worry about yourself; pray for others. Someone else will pray for you. When one part of the physical body is ill, the rest of the body compensates for it. The same kind of thing is true in the prayer life of the church body. The sick finger can't help itself; the rest of the body has to support it in its weakness. We must pray for each other.

The Cure That War Brings

D. Martyn Lloyd-Jones gave the following illustration about replacing the superfluous with the significant:

"Before the outbreak of the Spanish Civil War, in Barcelona, Madrid and other places, there were psychological clinics with large numbers of neurotics undergoing drug treatments and others attending regularly for psychoanalysis and such like. They had their personal problems, their worries, their anxieties, their temptations, having to go back week after week, month after month, to the clinics in order to be kept going. Then came the Civil War; and one of the first and most striking effects of that War was that it virtually emptied the psychological and psychiatric clinics. These neurotic people were suddenly cured by a greater anxiety, the anxiety about their whole position, whether their homes would still be there, whether their husbands would still be alive, whether their children would be killed. Their greater anxieties got rid of the lesser ones. In having to give attention to the bigger problem they forgot their own personal and somewhat petty problems" (*The Christian Soldier: An Exposition of Ephesians 6:10 to 20* [Grand Rapids: Baker, 1978], p. 357). Do you want to be a healthy person? Then lose yourself in the things that matter—the spiritual battles of other people. Lose yourself in consuming prayer for the kingdom of God and you won't have trouble with your petty anxieties.

I think it's needful for us to learn that. One of the reasons people in our society are experiencing all kinds of psychologically-induced aches and pains is simple: We are totally self-centered. I consider myself to be somewhat patient, but it's hard for me to tolerate people who are totally consumed with their own problems. That is a manifestation of self-centeredness that is foreign to the Christian life. We should be so lost in the needs of others that self is not a big issue. Let your little anxieties give way to greater ones; the spiritual battles of others.

E. The Qualification for Prayer

The pervasive thought in Ephesians 6:18 is that we are to pray in the Spirit.

1. The meaning

Praying in the Spirit has nothing to do with speaking in tongues. Some people have tried to make that claim, but you cannot introduce speaking in tongues into this verse. Jude 20 refers to "praying in the Holy Spirit." Praying in the Spirit is the same as praying in the name of Christ— praying in a manner consistent with who He is and what His will is. Learn to pray in concert with the Spirit. Make your prayers a duet with the One who intercedes for you. Romans 8:26-27 says, "We know not what we should pray for as we ought; but the Spirit himself maketh intercession for us with groanings which cannot be uttered. And he [God] that searcheth the hearts knoweth what is the mind of the Spirit." He hears and answers. While you live the Christian life, the Spirit of God within you prays on your behalf. He always prays the right prayer and receives the right answer. That's why verse 28 says, "All things work together for good." That's not an accident. Praying in the Spirit is simply making your own prayers consistent with the mind and the will of the Spirit.

2. The method

How do you make your prayers consistent with the Spirit? By walking in the fullness of the Spirit. As your life is filled with the Spirit, as you walk in obedience to the Spirit, and as you are constantly communing with God, the Spirit of God will govern your thoughts so that your prayers will be in harmony with Him. What a tremendous thing it is to know that I can join my prayers with the Spirit of God and can cry Abba Father from the depths of my heart and know that He hears and answers: The one pervasive goal of our prayer life shoud be to pray in the Spirit. Zechariah 12:10 calls the Holy Spirit "the Spirit of grace and of supplications." That's no different than praying in Jesus' name. In Galatians 4:6 the Holy Spirit is called "the Spirit of his [the Father's] Son." Our lives are to be an open communion with God.

II. THE SPECIFIC ILLUSTRATION (vv. 19-24)

A. The Intention (vv. 19-20)

"And for me, that utterance may be given unto me, that I may open my mouth boldly to make known the mystery of the gospel, for which I am an ambassador in bonds; that in this I may speak boldly, as I ought to speak."

Paul himself is the illustration. He didn't want prayer for his physical needs but for his spiritual battle. He wanted prayer that God would allow him to be bold, courageous, and straightforward in his speech. Paul was facing the enemy while he was a prisoner in Rome. Secular ambassadors have diplomatic immunity, but not this spiritual "ambassador"— he was chained. The battle was tough. He asked for prayer. We need to pray for our leaders, for our preachers.

People say, "Why do we need to pray for preachers? Who needs to pray for someone like Paul? He has his life together. We have to pray for the people on the periphery." But remember this: If the guy in the lead falls, many of the people following him are going to fall with him. Paul knew that the followers were only as strong as their leaders. Paul wanted prayer for boldness in his speaking. He knew his boldness might cause others to be bold. In Philippians 1:14 he says that his imprisonment gave greater boldness to others. As they prayed for him, he became a stronger example. That helped them. Paul wanted them to pray for a spiritual battle to be won.

B. The Information (vv. 21-22)

1. Communication (v. 21)

"But that ye also may know my affairs, and how I do, Tychicus, a beloved brother and faithful minister in the Lord, shall make known to you all things."

Paul didn't expect the Ephesians to pray for him without information, so he sent them his good friend Tychicus. He is mentioned five times in the New Testament. He delivered the letter to the Ephesians and brought word about Paul because they were concerned. They didn't know what was happening in his life. They didn't know what it was like for him in prison. Paul wanted them to be able to pray intelligently.

2. Comfort (v. 22)

"Whom I have sent unto you for the same purpose, that ye might know our affairs, and that he might comfort your hearts."

If we're going to pray, let's pray about spiritual things and open up our lives to each other so we have something to pray about. We have to communicate. We have to share the battle and the victories so we can carry others' cares. We are to be God-conscious, selfless, watchful, Spirit-filled, persistent, and bold as we seek God's glory in our prayers. When we live that kind of life and pray those kind of prayers, we'll be more like Jesus Christ. As we pray for each other, the body will be built up and God will be glorified.

C. The Invocation (vv. 23-24)

"Peace be to the brethren, and love with faith, from God, the Father, and the Lord Jesus Christ. Grace be with all them that love our Lord Jesus Christ in sincerity. Amen."

Focusing on the Facts

1. What is the closing theme of the book of Ephesians (Eph. 6:18; see p. 189)?
2. In what way is prayer a part of the Christian armor (see p. 189)?
3. Explain how prayer is like breathing (see p. 189).
4. List some of the resources that the book of Ephesians describes as belonging to the Christian (see pp. 190-91).
5. What problem can surface once a believer is aware of the tremendous resources he has been given (1 Cor. 10:12; see p. 191)?
6. When are Christians to pray (Eph. 6:18; see p. 192)?
7. Describe the pattern for prayer that the New Testament gives (see pp. 192-93).
8. What does it mean to pray at all times (see p. 193)?
9. What does it mean to "continue in prayer" (Col. 4:2; see p. 194)?
10. What was Christ's purpose in telling the stories in Luke 11:5-10 and Luke 18:1-8 (see p. 194)?
11. Define "prayer" and "supplication" (see p. 195).
12. What are the different ways you can pray (see p. 195)?
13. What time of day should we pray (see p. 195)?
14. Which is more important: prayer or knowledge? Why (see p. 196)?
15. Why should Christians watch with all perseverance and supplication (Eph. 6:18; see p. 197)?
16. What are three guidelines that should mark our prayers? Explain each one (see pp. 197-98).
17. What did Paul want the Ephesians to pray for on his behalf (Eph. 6:19; see p. 199)?

18. Whom are the indirect objects of our prayers? Explain (Eph. 6:18; see p. 199).
19. What does it mean to pray in the Spirit (Eph. 6:18; see p. 201)?
20. How can you pray in the Spirit (see p. 201)?
21. Why is it important to pray for your spiritual leaders (see p. 202)?

Pondering the Principles

1. Read 1 Corinthians 10:12. Does that verse convict you? Do you find you don't often acknowledge God for what He has done in your life? Review the resources that God has given you (see (pp. 190-91). Are you guilty of taking all those things for granted? If you are, remedy that problem right now. Ask God to forgive you of your self-sufficiency. Ask Him to bring the kinds of things into your life that will cause you to depend on Him. Thank Him for all the resources He has given you. Thank Him for all He is doing for you now and will do for you in the future.

2. Read Colossians 3:1-4. Verse 1 indicates that as a Christian, you are risen with Christ, positionally. That should have a profound effect on how you live. According to verses 1-2, what is your responsibility? Are you fulfilling that responsibility? According to verse 3, why should you fulfill your responsibility? According to verse 4, what is the ultimate purpose of your actions? If you are not fulfilling the exhortation that Paul gives, how can you expect to have a beneficial prayer life? Be devoted to being heavenly minded—and earthly good!

3. There are three guidelines that are important for you to follow when you pray (see pp. 192-94). Do you pray specifically? If you don't, begin to find out specific needs you can pray for so you can give God glory for His answers. Do you pray more for others or for yourself? If you pray more for yourself, leave your selfishness behind and concentrate on the needs of others. Trust God to care for your needs and remember that others are praying for you. Do you pray more for people's physical needs or their spiritual needs? If you pray more for their physical needs, reevaluate your priorities in prayer. By all means continue to pray for physical needs, but begin to concentrate more on spiritual needs. Pray that others will experience more victories over Satan's assaults in the daily battle.

4. When you pray, are you asking God for the kinds of things that are consistent with His will for your life and the lives of others? If you're not, then you're not praying in the Spirit. Seek to be filled with the Spirit. Absorb yourself in God's Word so you can get to know the mind of the Spirit. Walk in obedience to the

commands of Scripture and you will find yourself becoming more in tune with the Holy Spirit's guidance of your life. Thank God for giving you the Spirit.

12
Principles for Powerful Living

Outline

Introduction
A. The Purpose of the Letter to Corinth
B. The Key to the Letter to Corinth

Lesson
I. Be Alert
   A. The Positive Principle
      1. The physical sense
      2. The spiritual sense
   B. The Negative Situation
      1. The symptoms
         a) Physical stupor
         b) Spiritual stupor
      2. The disease
   C. The New Testament Injunctions
      1. Watch for Satan
      2. Watch for temptation
      3. Watch for apathy
      4. Watch for false teachers
      5. Watch in prayer
      6. Watch for the Lord's return
   D. The Practical Application
II. Be Firm
   A. The Positive Principle
   B. The Negative Situation
      1. Denying God's revelation
         a) Foolishness
         b) Deception
      2. Denying the person of Christ
         a) Committing cultic practices
         b) Being carried away by idols
         c) Cursing Jesus

Introduction

First Corinthians 16:13-14 says, "Watch, stand fast in the faith, [act] like men, be strong. Let all your things be done with love." That is a short text, but it is loaded with things we need to understand. We are going to see five imperatives that I call "Principles for Powerful Living."

A. The Purpose of the Letter to Corinth

Of all the churches to which Paul wrote, none was in as much trouble, was as sinful, or had failed to meet God's design as completely as the Corinthian church. Therefore, it received the greatest amount of rebuke. At the same time, Paul's words show evidence of his love for them, because love admonishes and rebukes visible sin. If you add the sixteen chapters of 1 Corinthians to the thirteen chapters of 2 Corinthians they total twenty-nine chapters—all written to straighten out one church. If combined, they would make the longest book in the New Testament. I would prefer not to have that many chapters written to me to straighten me out. But that's what happened to Corinth. The book is loaded with rebuke, but it is also laden with love because love calls us to righteousness.

B. The Key to the Letter to Corinth

The key to the letters to Corinth is 1 Corinthians 4:14: "I write not these things to shame you, but as my beloved sons I warn you." The letters were not written to shame the Corinthians; they were written out of love to admonish them to righteous behavior so they could begin to enjoy the blessings of God. First Corinthians is a love book that comes to a peak in chapter 13 with a great definition of love. Paul rebukes the Corinthians, but his is a rebuke of love. He wants to shake them out of their sinfulness, so he tackles every problem they had.

In 1 Corinthians, Paul writes fourteen chapters to straighten out their errant behavior, one chapter to straighten out their errant theology, and one chapter to close his thoughts. But what jumps out of the last chapter are the imperatives in verses 13 and 14. There are five of them. They are commands, not options. The Holy Spirit makes demands on the believer. As I studied these five imperatives, I found that they are the positive side of all the negatives that Paul talked about in the first fifteen chapters. Paul gives the Corinthians five commands: Watch, stand fast in the faith, act like men, be strengthened, and do everything in love. If they had responded to those five things, there would have been no need to write the rest of the book. These five things can reverse the errors in your life.

Lesson

I. BE ALERT (v. 13*a*)

   A. The Positive Principle

The word "watch" in the Greek language is *grēgoreō* from which the English derives the name Gregory. It means "to be alert."

     1. The physical sense

The word can be used in a physical sense, such as being awake as opposed to being asleep. First Thessalonians 5:10 says, "[Christ] died for us that, whether we wake or sleep, we should live together with him." The word translated "wake" means alive as opposed to dead in the context of the passage.

     2. The spiritual sense

First Thessalonians 5:6 says, "Therefore, let us not sleep, as do others, but let us watch and be sober-minded."

The word translated "watch" could be used of a physical awakening or a spiritual awakening. In 1 Corinthians 16:13 Paul uses it in a spiritual sense. He is not writing to people who are sound asleep physically, but to those who are asleep spiritually. He says, "Wake up! Be alert!" According to most lexicons, "watch" means more than just being awake as opposed to asleep; it means a determined effort to be awake and aware. Incidentally, *grēgoreō* is used twenty-two other times in the New Testament, often in reference to the Christian life. We have to be alert to understand and evaluate what the adversary is doing. Paul is saying that you can't live the Christian life in a state of stupor; you have to be alert.

   B. The Negative Situation

The Corinthians were in a stupor all the time.

     1. The symptoms

       a) Physical stupor

The Corinthians were often drunk. First Corinthians 11:20-21 says, "When ye come together, therefore, into one place, this is not to eat the Lord's supper. For in eating everyone taketh before the other his own supper; and one is hungry, and another is drunk." They were getting drunk. One of the reasons for not getting drunk is that when you are drunk, you are no longer alert to what's going on in your life. You are not alert to Satan, temptation, or people's needs. That's a good reason never to take anything that will bring you under its power and blind you from being alert.

b) Spiritual stupor

Paul's main emphasis is that the Corinthians were not alert to spiritual things. That is a deadly problem for a Christian. In various churches where the Bible isn't taught, Christians don't understand spiritual principles. They live most of their lives in a stupor. If you tell them some simple spiritual truth, they respond as if it's been dropped out of heaven right then.

As we look at each of the five commands in 1 Corinthians 16:13-14, I want to show you the opposite situation, which was taking place in Corinth. Were the Corinthians alert? No.

(1) 1 Corinthians 5:6—"Know ye not that a little leaven leaveneth the whole lump?" Paul was saying, "Don't you know that you can't let sinners in the fellowship without them effecting it?"

(2) 1 Corinthians 5:12—"Do not ye judge them that are within?" In other words, "Don't you evaluate people to determine if they are a plus to your fellowship?"

(3) 1 Corinthians 6:2—"Do ye not know that the saints shall judge the world?" Paul is saying, "Take care of your matters in the way that God has granted you authority to do rather than taking them before a pagan judge."

(4) 1 Corinthians 6:3—"Know ye not that we shall judge angels?" In other words, "Don't you know what a high calling we have before God? We ought to be able to settle our own problems."

(5) 1 Corinthians 6:5—"Is it so, that there is not a wise man among you?"

(6) 1 Corinthians 6:9—"Know ye not that the unrighteous shall not inherit the kingdom of God?"

(7) 1 Corinthians 6:15—"Know ye not that your bodies are the members of Christ?"

(8) 1 Corinthians 6:16—"Know ye not that he who is joined to an harlot is one body?"

(9) 1 Corinthians 6:19—"Know ye not that your body is the temple of the Holy Spirit?"

2. The disease

The problem with the Corinthians was that they didn't know. You can't be alert if you don't know anything. They were in a spiritual stupor. That's why 1 Corinthians 8:9 and 10:12 say, "Take heed." First Corinthians 12:1 says, "Now concerning spiritual gifts, brethren, I would not have you ignorant." But they were ignorant. They weren't alert. The result was that their lives were messed up. Part of the Corinthian problem can be summed up in 1 Corinthians 6:12: "All things are lawful unto me, but all things are not expedient; all things are lawful for me, but I will not be brought under the power of any." Since the Corinthians were in such a stupor, they were brought under the power of everything—every phony human philosophy, every wrong kind of human behavior— because they weren't alert.

You say, "But they didn't have resources." They had plenty of resources. That's why 1 Corinthians 15:34 says, "Awake to righteousness, and sin not." The believer has to be alert. You will never experience victory in the Christian life by being ignorant. You will never follow principles you don't know. You will have forfeited the joy of being in the will of God and enjoying the blessing of God.

C. The New Testament Injunctions

What are we to watch for?

1. Watch for Satan

In 1 Peter 5:8 Peter says, "Be sober, be vigilant, because your adversary, the devil, like a roaring lion walketh about, seeking whom he may devour." Whom will he devour? The one who's not watching. You need to be alert to the wily and crafty subtleties of Satan. You need to understand how he operates. He is like a football coach with only three plays: the lust of the flesh, the lust of the eyes, and the pride of life (1 John 2:16). You know his offensive plays; they ought to be easy to defend against. You need to learn the enemy's strategies. Don't get trapped, because he's looking for the one who's off guard.

2. Watch for temptation

   In Mark 14:38 Jesus says, "Watch ye and pray, lest ye enter into temptation." Satan has temptations you've never even thought of. You can't blithely expose yourself to everything in the world without having it affect you. Temptation will hurt you, so keep your eyes open.

3. Watch for apathy

   When Christ speaks to the church at Sardis in Revelation 3:1-2, He says, "Thou hast a name that thou livest, and art dead. Be watchful, and strengthen the things which remain." A church can become apathetic. A Christian can become smug, self-content, and indifferent. The Lord then said, "I will come on thee as a thief, and thou shalt not know what hour I will come" (Rev. 3:3). The Lord will chasten an apathetic, indifferent Christian who doesn't deal with his sin, weakness, and disobedience. Don't think you can do your own thing without any consequence. I believe God will chasten you because He is a loving God who wants to lead you to proper behavior. He wants to pour out all His blessings on you. You need to watch for apathy in your life. When you get comfortable with your sin and are no longer trying to deal with it, you're in trouble.

4. Watch for false teachers

   In writing to Timothy, Paul said people would come who would not teach sound doctrine. They would turn the ears of the people away from the truth to fables (2 Tim. 4:3-4). In verse 5 Paul says, "Watch thou." You need to be aware of false teaching. Keep your mind alert.

5. Watch in prayer

   Peter says, "Watch unto prayer" (1 Pet. 4:7). In Ephesians 6:18 Paul says we're to be "praying always with all prayer and supplication in the Spirit, and watching thereunto with all perseverance." God wants you to pray about specific issues. But how can you pray if you don't know what's going on?

6. Watch for the Lord's return

   Matthew 25:13 says, "Watch, therefore; for ye know neither the day nor the hour in which the Son of man cometh" (cf. Matt. 24:42). What does it mean to watch? It doesn't mean watch the sky; it means watch your life.

213

You only have so much time to do what God has given you to do, so watch.

The Corinthians missed their opportunity. They were not alert. Consequently, they were victimized by Satan, temptation, apathy, false teachers, and prayerlessness. They were not ready for the Lord's return. They even denied the resurrection (1 Cor. 15:12). So Paul informs them that they could reverse their behavior if they became alert.

D. The Practical Application

You ask, "How do you become alert?" All the warnings you need to know are in the Word of God. To watch, just look in the Bible. It is like a microscope that magnifies every subtlety of Satan. It reveals all. Watch by looking in the Bible and then apply the principles. The Word of God "is profitable for doctrine, for reproof, for correction, for instruction in righteousness, that the man of God may be perfect" (2 Tim. 3:16-17).

II. BE FIRM (v. 13b)

I like people who are firm—who stand for what they believe. I don't like people who blow with the wind. I like people who hold to what they believe.

A. The Positive Principle

Paul says, "Stand fast in the faith." The Greek word for "stand fast" is stēkō and refers to being rooted. Commentator Charles Hodge says, "Don't consider every point of doctrine an open question" (*An Exposition of the First Epistle to the Corinthians* [Grand Rapids: Eerdmans, 1974], p. 369). The Corinthians were blowing with the breeze.

The "faith" Paul was referring to was faith in the content of God's revelation. We're to stand fast in the gospel. Jude 3 says, "Earnestly contend for the faith which was once delivered unto the saints." Christianity is the faith. First Timothy 6:12 says, "Fight the good fight of faith." But that's not the best translation. It should say, "Fight the good fight of *the* faith." We need to fight to hold on to the faith because Satan wants to take it away from us.

B. The Negative Situation

The Corinthians weren't holding onto the faith. Our faith in the content of the gospel is supernaturally revealed by God.

It has no equal. In a sense, the Corinthians had even let go of that.

1. Denying God's revelation

    a) Foolishness

    The Corinthians were saying the Christian faith was foolishness. First Corinthians 1:18 says, "For the preaching of the cross is to them that perish foolishness." It is foolishness to all the wise people, scribes, and disputers of this age who elevate human wisdom (v. 20). Paul calls it the wisdom of the world (v. 21). The gospel is a stumbling block to them.

    The Corinthians had allowed human wisdom to so infest the church that they were accepting it on an equal basis with God's revelation. They allowed God's revelation to lose its distinctiveness. They had dragged human philosophies into the assembly, mixing those philosophies with God's truth. That can't be done because they are not on the same level. God's revelation is not equal with human wisdom; it surpasses it. The Corinthians were tearing at the heart of Christianity by toying with the idea that human philosophy was compatible with God's revelation.

    b) Deception

    In 1 Corinthians 3:18 Paul says, "Let no man deceive himself. If any man among you seemeth to be wise in this age, let him become a fool, that he may be wise." In other words, if you think you're really smart, you aren't. When you subtract human wisdom, true wisdom is left. Don't be deceiving yourselves. The Corinthians had deceived themselves into thinking that human wisdom was on an equal level with God's revelation. People today think the Bible is simply a human commentary on a view of God that existed in the time in which it was written.

2. Denying the person of Christ

    The second greatest feature of Christianity after God's revelation is the person of Christ. You should stand fast in who He is.

    a) Committing cultic practices

The Corinthians had given themselves over to a mixture of paganism and Christianity. They dragged many of their cultic practices into the assembly. They had allowed pagan ecstasies, trances, and other things from their cultural religion to come into the church. When they met together, there were some people who truly ministered in the Lord and in His Spirit while others were supposedly ministering in some kind of ecstatic state. That was nothing but pure paganism.

b) Being carried away by idols

First Corinthians 12:2 says, "Ye know that ye were Gentiles [Gk., *ethnē*, 'heathen'], carried away unto these dumb idols, even as ye were led," The terminology Paul uses refers to being carried away in an ecstatic fashion—carried away like someone in a spiritual trance. Paul is saying, "You used to be led into ecstasies when you worshiped dumb idols, but now you're letting that happen in the assembly."

c) Cursing Jesus

In verse 3 Paul says, "No man speaking by the Spirit of God calleth Jesus accursed." There were people in the assembly who were standing up in the midst of their ecstasies—supposedly under the inspiration of the Holy Spirit—and cursing Jesus.

The Corinthians were not standing fast in the faith when they were undermining the authority of the Word of God and cursing Jesus; they were attacking Christianity at its heart.

3. Denying the resurrection

In 1 Corinthians 15:12 Paul says, "Now if Christ be preached that he rose from the dead, how say some among you that there is no resurrection of the dead?"

The Corinthians weren't standing in the faith. So when Paul says, "Stand fast in the faith," he was telling them to go back to the authority of the Word of God, the person of Christ, and the resurrection—the great cornerstone of Christianity.

C. The New Testament Injunctions

The New Testament has a lot to say about being firm.

1. Be firm in devotion to Christ

Philippians 4:1 says, "Stand fast in the Lord." Be firm in your commitment to Christ and believe in His resources.

2. Be firm in unity

Philippians 1:27 says, "Stand fast in one spirit."

3. Be firm in liberty

Galations 5:1 says, "Stand fast, therefore, in the liberty with which Christ hath made us free, and be not entangled again with the yoke of bondage."

4. Be firm in the will of God

Paul's co-worker Epaphras prayed that the Colossians might "stand perfect and complete in all the will of God" (Col. 4:12).

5. Be firm against Satan

Ephesians 6:10 says, "Be strong in the Lord." Verse 12 says, "For we wrestle not against flesh and blood." Then verse 13 says, "And having done all, to stand."

We are not to be blown about "with every wind of doctrine" (Eph. 4:14), or to give "heed to seducing spirits, and doctrines of demons" (1 Tim. 4:1). The Corinthians weren't firm or alert. They weren't studying the Word enough.

D. The Practical Application

The Bible tells us to be firm—to stand for the faith. Second Thessalonians 2:14-15 says, "[God] called you by our gospel, to the obtaining of the glory of our Lord Jesus Christ. Therefore, brethren, stand fast, and hold the traditions which ye have been taught, whether by word or our epistle." The key to being firm is the Word of God. If you're going to be alert, you have to look into the Word. If you're going to be firm, you have to know doctrine.

III. BE MATURE (v. 13c)

A. The Positive Principle

First Corinthians 16:13 says, "Act like men" (NASB). This is the only place in the New Testament where the Greek word translated "act" is used. The word is often translated "be of good courage" in the Septuagint. It refers to courage, but it can also refer to maturity. Both references can be considered equal. For example, an immature child tends not to be courageous while a mature person tends to be courageous. A child tends to be fearful while a mature person tends to have a sense of control and confidence. Paul was telling the Corinthians to be courageous, mature men. One way to translate the Greek word *andrizō* is "manly conduct." But I do want to emphasize the maturity element because courage follows maturity.

B. The Negative Situation

1. 1 Corinthians 14:20—"Brethren, be not children in understanding; however, in malice be ye children, but in understanding be men." Grow up!

2. 1 Corinthians 4:14, 21—Paul had to talk to the Corinthians like sons, and he had to treat them like little kids. If they didn't straighten up, he said, "Shall I come come unto you with a rod?" (v. 21). They were babies. They were not men in understanding, courage, and maturity. They were fighting, squabbling, immature babies floating from one false doctrine to another. Consequently, they could not defend themselves against the onslaughts of Satan.

3. 1 Corinthians 3:1-2—"And I, brethren, could not speak unto you as unto spiritual, but as unto carnal, even as unto babes in Christ. I have fed you with milk, and not with solid food; for to this time ye were not able to bear it, neither yet now are ye able." They were like babies. He couldn't give them solid food; he had to keep giving them milk.

The Corinthians had not grown up. They had to be dealt with like children and be spanked. Sibling rivalries had even started. They were taking brothers to court. Paul said, "When I was a child, I spoke as a child, I understood as a child, I thought as a child; but when I became a man, I put away childish things" (1 Cor. 13:11). Even their religious worship was infantile: It was all based on feelings and emotions rather than on truth and doctrine.

If the Corinthians had grown up, they would have eliminated many problems, including carnality and an infantile religion.

Their emotions should have given way to a contemplation of the truth by men of understanding. That's why I believe that the teaching of the Word of God, the music the church presents, and the structure of the church should always appeal to the highest level. That brings people to maturity. Feelings and emotions are at the infantile level. If the Corinthians had been alert, they wouldn't have had so many problems. If they had been firm, they would have been communicating their theology. If they had been mature, they would have eliminated their squabbles and immaturity.

C. The New Testament Injunctions

Everyone is to be mature.

1. 2 Peter 3:18—"But grow in grace, and in the knowledge of our Lord and Savior, Jesus Christ."

2. Ephesians 4:13-14—"Till we all come . . . unto the measure of the stature of the fullness of Christ; that we henceforth be no more children."

D. The Practical Application

You say, "To be alert I have to look through the Word. To be firm I have to know doctrine. But how can I grow up?" Peter says, "As newborn babes, desire the pure milk of the word, that ye may grow by it" (1 Pet. 2:2). Get in the Word and you'll find out that you'll be alert, firm, and will begin to mature.

IV. BE STRENGTHENED (v. 13d)

A. The Positive Principle

The Greek verb for "be strong" is in the passive voice, and literally means "be strengthened." You can't strengthen yourself; that's something the Lord has to do.

1. Ephesians 6:10—"Be strong in the Lord, and in the power of his might."

2. Luke 2:40—"And the child [Jesus] grew, and became strong in spirit." The Greek word for *strengthen* in this context implies a strengthening of the spirit, or a strong inner man that can overcome the flesh.

3. 2 Timothy 2:1—"Thou, therefore, my son, be strong in the grace that is in Christ Jesus." A strong spirit overcomes the flesh.

B. The Negative Situation

The Corinthians were not strengthened—their flesh ruled. Whatever the flesh told them to do, they did it. Paul told them they were carnal—victims of the flesh. But they thought they were strong. According to 1 Corinthians 4:18, they thought Paul would be afraid to face them. But in 1 Corinthians 10:12 Paul says, "Let him that thinketh he standeth take heed lest he fall." They thought they were strong, but they weren't.

1. The analysis

   a) A criticism of the Corinthians

   Paul told them they were puffed up (1 Cor. 4:6, 18; 5:2). They thought they were strong, spiritual superstars. In 1 Corinthians 4:7 Paul says, "For who maketh thee to differ from another? And what hast thou that thou didst not receive? Now if thou didst receive it, why dost thou glory, as if thou hadst not received it?" In other words, "What makes you think you're so hot? If you're different from others, God made you that way. If you have anything, God gave it to you; it had nothing to do with you."

   In verse 8 Paul becomes sarcastic, "Now ye are full, now ye are rich, ye have reigned as kings without us; I would to God ye did reign."

   b) A comparison with the apostles

   In verse 9-10 Paul says, "For I think that God hath set forth us, the apostles, last, as it were appointed to death; for we are made a spectacle unto the world, and to angels, and to men. We are fools for Christ's sake, but ye are wise in Christ; we are weak, but ye are strong; ye are honorable, but we are despised." The Corinthians were so proud that they were looking down from their vantage point on the apostles. In verses 11-13 Paul says, "Even unto this present hour we both hunger, and thirst, and are naked, and are buffeted, and have no certain dwelling place; and labor, working with our own hands. Being reviled, we bless; being persecuted; we endure it; being defamed, we entreat; we are made as the filth of the world, and are the offscouring of all things." They didn't realize that Paul was saying true greatness comes through true humility. When we're weak, then we're strong (2 Cor. 12:10). They thought they were so strong, but they weren't strong at all.

2. The abuse

The Corinthians were so weak spiritually that they actually became weak physically. First Corinthians 11:30 says that as a result of spiritual weakness and the mistreatment of sacred things, "many are weak and sickly among you, and many sleep." Their spiritual weakness brought about physical weakness, disease, and death. They thought they were strong, but they were weak.

3. The admonition

In 1 Corinthians 9:24 Paul reminds them that the Christian life is a race. If they were going to win it, they would have to run. In verse 25 he says, "Every man that striveth for the mastery is temperate in all things." You can't live the Christian life in a halfhearted manner. If you're going to run to win, you're going to have to discipline yourself. Then Paul says, "I keep under my body, and bring it into subjection" (v. 27). The undisciplined and weak Corinthians thought they were so strong that they could indulge themselves with no concern for man or God. But Paul says, "No. You have to be engaged in a life of self-denial, self-sacrifice, and self-discipline."

C. The New Testament Injunctions

1. Be strong against Satan (Eph. 6:10-11)

2. Be strong in service (Phil. 4:13)

Paul said, "I can do all things through Christ, who strengtheneth me." He was talking about his ministry and service.

3. Be strong in good works (Col. 1:10-11)

We are strengthened to do good works. Daniel 11:32 says, "The people that do know their God shall be strong, and do exploits."

D. The Practical Application

You ask, "I am being made alert, firm, and mature through the Word, but how can I be strong?" Strength comes from another source. Psalm 27:14 says, "Wait on the Lord; be of good courage, and he shall strengthen thine heart. Wait, I say, on the Lord." Who is the one who gives us strength? The Lord. Ephesians 6:10 says, "Be strong in the Lord, and in the power of his might." You say, "But how does the Lord strengthen me?" By His Holy Spirit. Ephesians 3:16 says we are "to be strengthened with might by his Spirit in the inner man." As you yield your life to the Spirit of God, you will be strengthened by His strength. True strength is from God by His Spirit. As you yield to the Spirit, He strengthens you. If you get into the Word and yield to the Spirit, you'll be alert, firm, mature, and strengthened.

V. BE LOVING (v. 14)

This last principle is important because it balances the other four. If we only had those four, we might become militant in the world. So verse 14 says, "Let all your things be done with love."

A. The Positive Principle

We have received our marching orders, we're ready for battle, and we've been given four commands, but then Paul says, "By the way, I want all of you to have an attitude of love." That's the beautiful principle: unretreating courage and unfailing love. They have to be side-by-side. If you have too much love and not enough doctrine, you will be washed away by sentimentalism. If you have too much doctrine and not enough love, you will be a harsh theologian. You've got to have both love and sound doctrine.

B. The Negative Situation

The Corinthians were not loving.

1. They were fighting each other. According to 1 Corinthians 1:10 there were divisions [Gk., *schismata*] among them. In 1 Corinthians 3:4 Paul says, "One saith, I am of Paul; and another, I am of Apollos; are ye not carnal?"

2. In 1 Corinthians 5:1 Paul accuses the Corinthians of perverting their love and acting immorally. Someone had even defiled the wife of his father. Then in 1 Corinthians 6:16 Paul accuses them of joining themselves to harlots. They had perverted the whole concept of love.

3. According to 1 Corinthians 6:1-8 they were suing each other.

4. According to 1 Corinthians 7:1-7 marriage partners were depriving each other.

5. According to 1 Corinthians 8 stronger brothers were causing weaker brothers to stumble.

6. According to 1 Corinthians 11:17-22 they were hogging food at the Lord's love feast leaving the poor, who came late, nothing to eat.

7. According to 1 Corinthians 12, they had an unloving approach to spiritual gifts.

There was no love in their assembly. So Paul reverses their whole life-style in one statement: "Let all your things be done with love." Two things would straighten out their church: sound doctrine and love. If they had put those two things together, they would have reversed their behavior.

C. The New Testament Injunctions

We see sound doctrine and love together throughout the New Testament. Paul says, "Let all your things be done with love" (1 Cor. 16:14). By "love" Paul is referring to self-sacrificing service to one in need. It is not an emotion or feeling, but an act of service. Jesus said, "Love one another; as I have loved you" (John 13:34). The way Jesus showed He loved the disciples was by washing their feet (John 13:5). We show love by meeting someone's need.

D. The Practical Application

Where does love come from? In Ephesians 3 Paul prays that we will "be strengthened with might by His Spirit in the inner man . . . [and] know the love of Christ, which passeth knowledge" (vv. 16, 19). Love is from the Spirit. The Spirit and the Word work together to provide sound doctrine and love, making the believer into what God wants him to be.

Be alert, firm, mature, strengthened, and loving. Those are the principles for powerful living. They are generated by the Word and the Holy Spirit. They come together to make sound doctrine and love the two pillars that hold the church up. If we would follow 1 Corinthians 16:13-14, we won't have to be straightened out like the Corinthians were.

Focusing on the Facts

1. Explain why 1 Corinthians can be considered a book of rebuke and love (see p. 209).
2. Name the five imperatives from 1 Corinthians 16:13-14. What would have happened had the Corinthians followed them (see p. 209)?
3. What was Paul referring to when he told the Corinthians to watch (1 Cor. 16:13; see p. 210)?

4. Explain the physical stupor that was a problem with some of the Corinthians (1 Cor. 11:20-21). Explain their spiritual stupor. Support your answer with Scripture (see pp. 210-11).
5. As a result of their spiritual stupor, what were the Corinthians controlled by (see p. 211)?
6. What are six things a Christian has to watch for? Explain each one (see pp. 212-13).
7. How does the Lord deal with an apathetic Christian (see p. 213)?
8. How do you become alert (2 Tim. 3:16-17; see p. 214)?
9. What does Paul mean by "stand fast in the faith" (1 Cor. 16:13; see p. 214)?
10. What three facts of Christianity had the Corinthians denied (see pp. 215-16)?
11. What were the Corinthians saying about the Christian faith (1 Cor. 1:18-20; see p. 215)?
12. What is the problem with putting God's revelation on the same level with human wisdom (see p. 215)?
13. Explain how the Corinthians were denying the person of Christ by their behavior (1 Cor. 12:1-3; see pp. 215-16).
14. What does the New Testament say about being firm (see p. 217)?
15. What is the key to being firm (2 Thess. 2:14-15; see p. 217)?
16. Explain how courage and maturity go together (see p. 218).
17. In what manner did Paul have to treat the Corinthians (1 Cor. 3:1-2; see p. 218)?
18. Give two Scripture verses that show the importance of being mature (see p. 219).
19. How does a Christian grow (1 Pet. 2:2; see p. 219)?
20. What did Paul tell the Corinthians was the way to true greatness (1 Cor. 4:9-13; see p. 220)?
21. What happened to some of the Corinthians as a result of their spiritual weakness (1 Cor. 11:30; see p. 221)?
22. In what ways are Christians to be strong (see p. 221)?
23. How can a Christian be strengthened (Eph. 3:16; see p. 222)?
24. What are two things that can happen when sound doctrine and love are out of balance (see p. 222)?
25. What were the Corinthians doing that showed they weren't loving (see pp. 222-23)?
26. Explain the New Testament concept of love (see p. 223).

Pondering the Principles

1. As a Christian there are several things you need to watch for. Do you watch for Satan and his subtle attacks? Do you watch for temptation so you can avoid it? Are you sensitive to any attitude

of indifference that could creep into your life? Are you careful to avoid false teachers? Are you looking out for the needs of others so you can pray for them? Are you careful to utilize your time so you will be ready for the Lord's return? If you are doing all those things, you won't be victimized. If you are not doing those things, begin to watch today.

2. Among the many problems the Corinthians had, they had denied God's revelation, the person of Christ, and the resurrection. Is there anything in your life that could cause someone to think you are denying one or more of those truths? If there is, ask God to reveal to you a greater understanding of His Word. In addition, examine your own commitment to Him. If you are not devoted to the Lord in all areas of your life, you will be susceptible to ungodly influences.

3. Paul tried to communicate to the Corinthians that true greatness comes through humility. Look up the following verses: Psalm 25:9; Prov. 15:33; Isa. 66:2; Matt. 5:3, 5; Luke 22:24-27; Phil. 2:3-11. In your own words, what does each of those passages say about humility? Are you on the path to true greatness? What areas in your life need to be conformed to scriptural humility? Beginning today, seek the Lord's guidance in conforming those areas to His will.

4. Is your love in balance with your knowledge of doctrine? Do you allow sentiment to rule over the clear commands of Scripture? Do you allow the letter of the law to rule over meeting a need someone has? Be careful to keep your obedience to Scripture and your commitment to love in balance.

Scripture Index

Moody Press, a ministry of the Moody Bible Institute, is designed for education, evangelization, and edification. If we may assist you in knowing more about Christ and the Christian life, please write us without obligation: Moody Press, c/o MLM, Chicago, Illinois 60610.